Tough Cookies

Tough Cookies

Leadership Lessons from 100 Years of the Girl Scouts

KATHY CLONINGER, CEO

Girl Scouts of the United States of America

with Fiona Soltes

WILEY

John Wiley & Sons, Inc.

ISBN: 978-1-118-00004-5 (cloth)
ISBN: 978-1-118-12963-0 (ebk)
ISBN: 978-1-118-12964-7 (ebk)
ISBN: 978-1-118-12962-3 (ebk)

Printed in the United States of America

10 9 8 7 6 5 4 3 2 1

CONTENTS

PREFACE

I'm on a plane, wearing my Girl Scout pin. The man in the next seat sees the pin and says, "Girl Scouts! Oh, yeah, Thin Mints!" Immediately I think two things: One is that it's great to work in an organization with such a visible, universal brand icon. The other is: "I wonder if he knows that the annual Girl Scout cookie sale is a unique and powerful $700 million education program that brings to life Girl Scouts' true brand: developing leadership in girls."

Like most folks, he doesn't know beans about that. All he wants to talk about is how good those Thin Mints taste.

It makes me want to write a book. . . .

ACKNOWLEDGMENTS

Heartfelt thanks to:

GSUSA Board Chair Connie Lindsey and former chairs Patricia Diaz Dennis and Cynthia Thompson. Their support and inspiration, their vision and partnership, and their courage to do what's right for girls during every tough step of the Girl Scout transformation kept all our heads high when our backs ached.

Fiona Soltes. Her ability to bring my thoughts and feelings to the written page and to propel me from "I don't have anything to say" to "Golly . . . we've got a book!" seems as amazing as everything we did at Girl Scouts.

Peter Johnston. With a big picture eye and wry humor that kept us all on task, he hatched this book project and managed it every step of the way.

Mike Williams. My dear husband's love and support and foot rubs and masterful editing—being CEO, let alone writing this book, would be beyond me if it weren't for him.

Sue Cloninger. My mother's leadership of my Girl Scout troop, from 1959 to 1963, is one of many millions of Girl Scout volunteer success stories. Many millions of girls, including me, thank each of those amazing women.

1 Leadership out of Balance

How well do we trust our leaders?

Not too well. A national survey[1] says nearly two-thirds of Americans think there is a leadership crisis in the country.

Not only do we doubt the abilities of those who make the nation's decisions, but we also fail to understand the mix of qualities that create great leadership, and the strengths that girls and women can contribute to that mix. (We might better understand if, for example, women—who make up half the population—were more than 3 percent of CEOs of Fortune 500 companies or more than 17 percent of the U.S. Congress.)

This book isn't a feminist "wo-manifesto." I'm not going to bluster about glass ceilings, old-boy networks, testosterone in corner offices, and the thin smokescreen of "You've come a long way, baby." Nor will this book play a blame game. I simply am going to look you in the eye and say that if the United States hopes to remain a major player among nations, facing challenges such as poverty, inadequate education, and global market competition, we're going to need to draw deeply from our entire talent pool, not just half of it.

---

[1] The 2010 *National Leadership Index,* an annual nationwide survey by Harvard's Kennedy School of Government and *U.S. News & World Report.*

For that to happen, we'll need a top-to-bottom overhaul of how the country views the leadership potential of girls and women. This book aims to impact your view about that, and to convince you, for the sake of our nation's leadership, that we need to invest strongly in our girls.

Cookies and Confidence

I've been involved in Girl Scout leadership for 27 years. Girl Scouting is a three-million-girl working model of how to unleash and develop the powerful potential of girls.

Which brings me back to the guy on the airplane, described in the Preface. Do you have any idea what it takes for a 10-year-old girl to go out and sell a thousand boxes of cookies, door to door? If you say, "Yeah, a strong mother!" you're missing the point. Of course Mom's support is essential to help each girl and protect her as she sells. But what's really going on when a girl sells all those cookies is this: she's learning to be an entrepreneur. She's learning business skills. She's learning teamwork. She's figuring out how to be organized. She's learning how to set and achieve goals. She's finding confidence in her ability to engage with people and convince them. She's developing strength as a person who Gets Things Done.

She is literally *discovering the leader in herself*. Out of her experience of planning her campaign and knocking on doors and looking people in the eye and making the sale, she emerges capable of amazing new things.

Few people outside of Girl Scouting realize this. A decade ago, when I was leading the Girl Scout council in middle

Tennessee, I engaged the Nashville Rotary Club to make the cookie sale part of the Rotary service project. The Rotarians signed up as business coaches for Girl Scouts who lived in a public housing community that's near where the downtown Rotarians meet. (People tend to think of Girl Scouts as being white, middle-class, and suburban. But we're every color America is, and we have troops in public housing, in prisons, in the inner cities, and on the prairies. We're in practically every zip code in the country. We're everywhere.)

The idea was that the Rotarians would meet with the girls, talk them through the project, and give them guidance based on their own business experience and expertise. We prepared for that meeting by using our Girl Scout cookie sale training program—the same one that we use with the girls—to train the Rotarians.

It blew them away. The Rotarians were astonished at how well our program taught basic business skills, salesmanship, financial literacy, goal setting, investing, and other abilities not usually associated with cute little girls. Several Rotarians told me later that the training program was more sophisticated than anything they'd ever used in their own companies.

Like practically everyone else in the United States (except Girl Scouts) the Rotarians hadn't taken the cookie sale seriously: after all, it was just something done by girls.

A Different Perspective

There's a real difference between the way the public looks at the accomplishments of girls and boys. People latch onto the cuteness and wholesomeness aspects of the cookie sale because

they really don't know what to do with the idea of girls act-
ing in an organized, effective, powerful way. And we in Girl
Scouting haven't yet done enough to publicize the fact that
the cookie sale is a huge leadership lesson for all involved, not
just an organizational fund-raiser with cute little girls on the
front lines to help boost sales.

For the girls, the cookie sale is a life-changing experience.
It is the only childhood activity available to girls ages 6 to
17 across the country that is actually a hands-on business.
It's not at all like reading about sales and merchandising in
a classroom. You literally, as a girl, are presented with the
chance to run your own business. And you do it like most
businesses, in partnership with a team.

Better yet, it's a business that people see as important. Just
being able to say "I'm a Girl Scout and I'm selling cookies"
puts a girl in a position of respect, influence, and approval. At
the same time, she's learning how to interact with coworkers,
how to play by rules, how to be ambitious, how hard work
pays off, and how to set both long-term and short-term goals.
The cookie sale is not just about how many boxes one girl
sells. It's about how many boxes the whole troop sells, and
what projects or field trips or adventures they'll all agree to
use the money for in the next year. The experience of the sale
is tangible; it validates a girl's worth.

Long-term goal setting? For eight-year-old kids, "next
year" is long-term goal setting. But many Girl Scouts dare to
plan further ahead than that. A friend told me a remarkable
story about her daughter, who joined Girl Scouts as a five-
year-old Daisy and stayed with the same troop all the way
through high school.

When the girls in the troop were in first or second grade, they decided that they wanted to go to London when they got to high school. They saved cookie-sale money every year, and they accomplished their goal. They went to London and visited the headquarters of the World Association of Girl Guides and Girl Scouts (WAGGGS is the international parent agency of Girl Scouts of the USA [GSUSA]), and they stayed at Pax Lodge, one of four world centers for Girl Guides and Girl Scouts. They came back feeling like citizens of the world. Nothing else in my daughter's life did as much to help her set big goals and learn to achieve them as the cookie sale.

Don't Blow Your Own Horn

One reason the guy on the airplane didn't understand the scope of the cookie sale was because no one had told him. Unlike boys, girls are seldom encouraged to highlight their own accomplishments.

For example, a national poll of American women[2] found that two-thirds of women of professional achievement, and more than three-fourths of those who were deemed "women of distinction," had been Girl Scouts in their youth. The same poll found that more than four out of five successful professional women who had been Girl Scouts rated their Girl Scout involvement as helping them achieve later success. Yet many women don't talk about their Girl Scout experience this way. A man is much more likely to list Boy Scouts on his résumé than a woman is to list Girl Scouts on hers. Some women don't link what they did as kids with their adult lives. Others value the Girl Scout experience personally, but

---

[2]*Defining Success,* Girl Scouts/Louis Harris & Associates, 1999.

they don't imagine that it's worth mentioning to anyone else. Women haven't been trained or inspired to talk about their own leadership development. A lot of them believe that if they do talk about it, no one will listen.

The Need for Change

Americans are uncomfortably aware that we need better leadership. So why don't we tap our whole talent pool instead of ignoring half of it?

An essential part of solving the leadership crisis that bedevils us is to bring more women into positions of leadership. That's not because women are better leaders than men. It's because men and women together make better leaders than either men or women can make by themselves.

If a blended leadership of men and women is best for the United States, then in order to achieve that blended leadership, some things are going to have to change. At Girl Scouts we have been thinking hard about the subject of major change. A few years ago we realized that Girl Scouting itself, facing a decline in membership and momentum, needed to change if we wanted to stay relevant in a world evolving "at the speed of girl." And so, in the most sweeping transformation in our hundred-year history, we turned a tradition-bound organization inside out.

This was no small task. Girl Scouts is one of the largest nonprofits in the country, with an annual operations budget of three-quarters of a billion dollars, and a million volunteers and nearly three million girls. Radically changing something that big is like having to tear down and rebuild an ocean liner sailing at full speed without sinking it. But we did it. We managed (and are still managing) to reinvent our ways of work, streamline our structures, build a new leadership brand, attract new public and private and corporate funding, and revitalize the fun and adventure a girl gains when she becomes a Girl Scout.

I'll explain the whole process as we go along, but briefly, we did it by going back to our roots: our core beliefs about who we are, what we do best, and why we're driven to do it. We also were driven by the belief that we were doing it to meet a huge unmet need, and that if we succeeded in revitalizing our own organization, we could lend a hand to improve our society as well.

The Message We Send

If we are to inspire girls toward leadership, we need to help girls change the way they see their own potential. Girls are growing up in a society that belittles their skills, their intelligence, and their abilities by telling them over and over that the only things about them that really matter to anybody are their looks and their sexuality. The top 25 TV shows for kids ages 12 to 17 regularly depict teen girls as highly sexualized and objectified.[3] In these shows, 98 percent of the sexual incidents involving underage females take place outside any kind of committed relationship. Three in four incidents are presented as being funny (not to the girls; to the other characters and to the audience). And in

---

[3]A recent study by the Parents Television Council.

these shows, 93 percent of the sexual incidents that involve young females are unhealthy, according to the American Psychological Association's definitions of healthy sexuality.

So what? Why should we care?

We should care because the message this stuff sends, regardless of how you feel about teen sexuality, is that girls are to be seen as sex objects first.

If that's how we're teaching teenage girls to see themselves, it's no wonder they seek confidence in how they look, and how desirable they are, above all else. "Today's girls view being sexy as the ultimate accolade," says Carol Platt Liebau, political analyst and commentator, and author of *Prude: How the Sex-Obsessed Culture Damages Girls (and America, Too!)* (Center Street, 2009). As a result, girls too often think the only way they can receive admiration is through promiscuity and sexual aggression.

What about admiring girls for expanding their horizons, growing in self-awareness, setting goals, using their intelligence, or taking on projects that help others? We don't see much encouragement for those values coming from our society's center, or its top or its grassroots. And if girls don't absorb those values as adolescents, it's going to be difficult for them to model those values when they become adults and parents.

Some people think this situation is hopeless. I disagree! The challenges are real, and the outlook is grim if we keep going the way we are, but we do have solutions within our reach.

We Can Do This

You are a solution. I don't know if you're reading this book as a parent, a woman, someone interested in leadership, someone who pays attention to gender issues, or someone who wants to know how a famous nonprofit organization turned itself inside out. Whoever you are, you can help.

Americans generally value equality. We try to be fair and just in how we treat kids. So here's an idea for you. It may sound simplistic, but it's the solid truth, and it may be the most important thing I have to tell you:

What's good for girls is good for the country.

We all benefit when every citizen is valued: boys, girls, men, and women. We all benefit when there's a place for us all at the table, and leadership is shared. I'm convinced that the United States will gain competitive advantage, in how our economy runs and how our civil society is played out, when we have men and women sharing the problems and sharing the solutions.

For that to happen, we must make a major change in our culture. A culture is about behavior. It's about how people treat each other, what our shared values are, and how people are rewarded and recognized. Those cultural assets determine how we develop our leaders.

Most of us already have a general sense of how blended leadership works. If you grew up in a home where the decisions were made by your parents together, openly, each tempering and respecting the other, you know what that means. If you didn't grow up that way but had childhood friends who did, you know what it means. If you're lucky enough to have a true partnership in your own life, you know exactly what it means.

My message is not about how individual people should live. There are households and organizations run entirely by men or by women that run beautifully. I'm talking instead about finding and nurturing a balance of leadership strength in our whole culture. To talk about that, we'll need to speak of averages and statistics. Statistic number one is that the population is evenly split between men and women. After that, the splitting becomes less even; we'll get back to that in a minute.

What Numbers Tell Us

For us to have a conversation about balance in decision making, we need to talk about things you can measure. For example, if I say to you that there's a serious imbalance of power between men and women in the United States, you might think, "Oh, of course she's right," or "No, she's blowing smoke and everything's fine." But if I tell you that only 15 percent of corporate board positions are held by women, or that 17 percent of members of the U.S. House of Representatives and Senate are women, then we have something real to talk about.

(If you think Congress is making progress toward gender balance, consider this: there's been a 1 percent increase of women per election cycle in the past 30 years. At this rate, we'll reach parity in 400 years.)

The statistics on women in leadership, dismal though they may be, are not really the root problem. They're a symptom. The problem is a lack of balance. I believe we can correct that. And I'm not talking about a radical feminist agenda, or about quotas. I'm talking about a country that works better, a country where more of us feel happy and proud of our productivity as citizens.

I'm talking about making a better world for us and for our sons and daughters. We can do that together, you and I. Because when it comes to the crunch, we are tough cookies.

2 How I Got Here

Three Things That I Really Believe:

1. The world needs to be better than it is.
2. Part of making the world better involves new ways of dealing with girls and women.
3. Girl Scouting has useful ideas about what those new ways can be.

In Girl Scouts, we've developed a holistic approach to leadership for girls. It encourages discovering yourself, connecting with others, and taking action to make the world better.

To help you understand how that approach creates leaders, let me tell you about my personal career, which has gone through those same stages. I grew up in a Dallas family of more love than income. There was no college history in our family. Daddy worked in midlevel management at Sears. Mama was secretary/personnel administrator for the Internal Revenue Service (IRS) and later for the Bureau of Alcohol, Tobacco and Firearms. We three daughters were latchkey kids. We'd pack up in the morning and go to school, and in the afternoon we'd let ourselves back into the house and structure our own time until our parents finished work. When Mama got home, she would put on her comfortable shoes and fix dinner (often with Daddy's help), then clean up afterward and make sure we did our homework. It was sort of like *Ozzie and Harriet*.

I was able to join Girl Scouts in third grade because my mother volunteered to start a new troop. She was willing to do this in her "spare" time, and I'll never be able to thank her enough. Mama and I already were close, and the four years she was my troop leader brought us closer. Girl Scouting wasn't the center of my world (I didn't earn the Gold Award), but it was something I thoroughly enjoyed. It also was, and still is, one of the best activity options for girls of our family's income, who don't get to go to all-girls schools and fancy summer camps.

Continuous Learning

As senior year drew to a close in high school, my guidance counselor (a woman) came to our house and sat down with Daddy and Mama and me. "Let's talk about what Kathy is going to do after she graduates."

Academically, I ranked high in my class. If I had been a boy, the counselor might have advised college, a first in our family. But I was a girl. "Don't worry about college," the counselor said. "Go to a good secretarial school. Learn typing and shorthand and how to make tickler files."

I want to say loud and clear that it's an honorable and valuable career to be a good secretary. The world would grind to a halt without secretaries. I was optimistic as I enrolled in secretarial school right after graduation. But after a few weeks, as the course focused on walking with a book balanced on your head, I had the feeling this wasn't the path my life would take.

One thing I had not learned, up to that point, was to quash an inner voice that tells you to follow your gut instinct. When something inside says, "Hey, how about this?" I hadn't learned to shut down that feeling.

One night that summer, some friends and I went to a small folk music club called the Rubaiyat. After a few minutes in this unpretentious, homey performance room with its wooden chairs and threadbare carpet on the little stage, my gut instinct was saying, "This is a good place for you, Kathy." My friends got bored and urged, "Let's get out of here." I didn't want to leave. In the bathroom I found, above the washbasin, a hand-lettered sign: WAITRESS WANTED. I took it down and went to the owner of the place. Handing it to him, I said, "You just hired your new waitress."

He probably thought, "Yeah? Who is this kid?" But he had a sense of humor, and he gave me a chance. I dropped out of secretarial school and waitressed at the Rubaiyat for four years, loving every night of it. The Rubaiyat was a small, intimate, shoestring operation where the music, the friendly patrons, and the fascinating singers and pickers who passed through town from "out on the road" all contributed to a sense of independence that thrilled me.

The September after high school, I enrolled in a couple of community college courses, psychology and German, just because it felt interesting and fun to learn new things. Some of my friends were doing likewise. We were all working, and it was a struggle sometimes to get the studying and homework done, so we'd meet for breakfast before school and cheer each other on.

At that point I wasn't focused on getting a college degree, nor on any particular life plan. Life seemed to be pulling me along, and the pulls were intriguing enough to follow. One pull was in the direction of seeing women get more involved in politics. I worked on Sissy Farenthold's campaign for governor of Texas. We lost, but I learned a lot about politics, and about aiming high and recovering from defeat. (I didn't see myself going into politics. I was just a girl waiting tables and taking community college courses. The things that really energized me were working with people and helping them.)

The community college courses began to add up. Art history. English literature. Political science. A professor asked what my goals were, and he suggested I get a bachelor's degree. I enrolled at the University of Texas Health Science Center in Dallas and, six years after graduating from high school, earned a degree in rehabilitation counseling. (My big sister Linda also enrolled and graduated in the same class. This milestone sisters achievement has kept us close, and both interested in social issues, ever since.)

During those six years, I wasn't a college girl who worked nights to put herself through school. Instead, I was a working girl who took classes for the fun of learning. Each class tuition was paid for with tips from waitressing at the Rubaiyat or wages from the jobs that followed.[1] The learning was its own reward. A degree was icing on the cake. Somewhere in Mama and Daddy's special stuff, there's a photo of a young girl with a mortarboard on her head: she looks sort of surprised, and she's probably about to start reading another book.

---

[1] I strongly advise—except if you receive rude or really shoddy service—that you *always* tip your server 20 percent. You never know the goals someone may be striving toward.

One of the classes opened a door to doing volunteer work at a halfway house where mildly retarded, institutionalized women were brought into a residence where they could learn to live on their own. Soon I was hired there full-time as program director, designing and conducting activities that taught the women how to function in mainstream society.

After college graduation I worked two years with the Job Corps, helping disadvantaged young men become self-sustaining after their Job Corps training.

Three one-year contracts followed: jobs in corporate or state-sponsored social service. One position involved teaching people in their thirties and forties how to change careers and hone a new path, how to cooperate for success, and how to interview for jobs and write résumés—skills that came in handy for the rest of my own working life. (How did I learn those skills, in order to teach them? By reading books and flailing a lot.)

Next I ran a YWCA branch in the Dallas metroplex system and, a year later, transferred to run another. Through seven jobs in seven years, I was learning and using a kaleidoscope of skills in social service.

I also enrolled in a master's degree program on nights and weekends. At this time, colleges didn't offer master's degrees in nonprofit management. So I took courses in counseling and guidance and also business management, to hone skills in human relations and running nonprofits. That combination has served me well.

Each day was busy and exciting. After a while on the YWCA job, though, my philosophy about how to run YWCA programs grew to be at odds with the methods of the person who supervised all YWCA branches in the Dallas–Fort Worth metroplex. As I pondered how to deal with that obstacle, life took an unexpected turn.

A Gap in the Résumé

A year earlier, through a series of coincidences that defy "ships passing in the night," I reconnected with a singer-songwriter named Mike who used to play at the Rubaiyat. Mike now was traveling constantly, playing 150 concerts a year in colleges all over the country. We began spending time together whenever he came through the Dallas area. One day when I was in turmoil about what to do with the YWCA job, Mike called out of the blue:

"I'm retiring from the road at the end of May. I want you to quit your job and come with me on an all-expenses-paid trip to everywhere."

If you are forging a serious career path, you know the importance of steering clear of nutty side trips that create unexplainable chasms in your résumé. But my gut reaction to Mike's wild invitation was a resounding "Yes!"

In June, Mike and I took off camping all over the United States for three glorious months. (Confession: instead of resigning from the Y, I negotiated a three-month leave of absence.) When summer ended, Mike decided to stay with me rather than continue his rambling. We came back to Dallas and I resumed working at the YWCA and also driving 50 miles each way on Saturdays to East Texas State University (now Texas A&M) in Commerce, Texas, to finish the master's degree.

By Christmas, I had gotten the master's degree and, without knowing what the next career move might be, resigned from the Y. Mike and I spent the holiday in Key West, Florida. The island was so lovely that we rented an apartment and stayed four months. I did a volunteer stint on the naval base, working the crisis hotline.

The Hand of Fate, Part 1

What's next, Kathy? You're almost 32. You have no life plan or career goal. You've held a series of service-related jobs, each for about a year. That kind of job-to-job movement means one of two things to potential employers: either you can't hold a job or you're wringing the juice out of each job and looking for bigger challenges.

Mike and I returned to Dallas. I started reading want ads, and found one seeking someone to lead "a small nonprofit agency in northern Colorado." I responded, and flew to interview at what turned out to be the Mountain Prairie Girl Scout Council in Greeley, Colorado. They offered the job. Mike and I drove out there (roving musicians are fairly portable), and we moved into a tiny house with a woodstove and endured a winter where snow piled hip-high and the temperature stayed well below zero for weeks at a time. I spent the winter driving the frozen prairie in a Volkswagen Bug with a heater that didn't always work. My Girl Scout career began as a "trial by ice."

I knew nothing about Girl Scouts except that it had been fun to be one as a girl. The job of leading a small Girl Scout council serving northeast Colorado quickly began to change my life. I was expected to be part of that community's leadership, to be visible and active, to establish credibility, and to steward a bunch of girls and volunteers and staff members who didn't know me from a bar of soap. It was time to grow up.

Fortunately, Girl Scouts of the USA (GSUSA), headquartered in New York City, the parent organization for all Girl Scout councils, offered a great training course that taught new council leaders a whole raft of business skills. That training, and the job, really stretched me out, much as Girl Scout troop activities had stretched Mama and me out when I was a girl.

During this time, Frances Hesselbein was CEO of GSUSA. (She later founded and ran the Peter Drucker Foundation. It's now called the Leader to Leader Foundation and she still runs it, and she's hailed as America's most accomplished nonprofit leader.) Frances made a point of testing a few small-council leaders by inviting them to take part in national Girl Scout think tanks and committees. She took an interest in me and began to bring me along as a mentor.

After two years at the Mountain Prairie council, I moved to the West Coast to work as an independent consultant in a much bigger Girl Scout council. But that council was in crisis and my job got swept away in the turmoil. This was a shock; but it also was an important lesson in how to recover from mistakes. Effective leadership, I have learned, comes not from avoiding all mistakes, but from always stretching far enough to make them, learn from them, and recover to try again. If you're not making any mistakes, you're not trying hard enough.

Back to Dallas again. My participation on GSUSA national think tanks and committees opened a door for

GSUSA to hire me as a staff consultant traveling Kansas, Oklahoma, and Arkansas to give management help and resources to small Girl Scout councils. And in 1987, that experience led to becoming CEO of the midsize Girl Scout council in San Antonio. Using skills from the Colorado council job and quickly learning many more, I thrived in this new job and the council prospered.

Right Opportunity, Wrong Place

Then came a sideways venture that looked very promising at first but turned out to be another mistake—although, looking back, it was an essential link in the chain. Anyway, didn't some wag (maybe me) say, "If you aren't making any mistakes, you're not trying hard enough"?

In 1991 Frances Hesselbein called and said, "If you had a chance at the job of a lifetime, but it meant leaving Girl Scouts, would you take it?" I said yes, and a month later joined the W.K. Kellogg Foundation, in Battle Creek, Michigan, as a program officer in education grants. This big move (and big pay boost) onto the national stage of social service with a huge foundation meant working on cutting-edge grants in public school reform throughout the United States. It seemed a very attractive career change—at first.

Let me say that I tremendously respect the work of the Kellogg Foundation, and admire the people I worked with. Yet the fit didn't feel right for me. A hint of the reason might be the series of two dozen photos of the top figures in the foundation's history that lined the grand circular stairway at foundation headquarters. The staff called it "the old white men gallery." Some of those old white men became dear friends and inspired me, and the Kellogg Foundation has a great track record of honoring and celebrating diversity in its programs. But I missed working in a women-led, women-centered organization.

After a year, Mike said one day, "I see the light going out in your eyes." He wanted me to try to find work in Nashville, Tennessee, a great place for songwriters. But no job was available there. And then there was: just two months later, the CEO of the middle Tennessee Girl Scout council retired after 23 years in office.

Leaving Kellogg and going back to being a Girl Scout council CEO would mean a major pay cut and a return to local, not national work. But it absolutely felt like the right move. I got the job and we moved to Music City.

And we loved it there. For 10 years I led Girl Scouting in a council that served nearly 20,000 girls in 38 counties of Tennessee. The job brought fulfilling work, great friends, good business and civic contacts, and lots of fun for music junkies like Mike and me in the country music capital of the world. Life was sweet. I expected to stay there until retirement.

The Hand of Fate, Part 2

In autumn 2002, the national CEO of Girl Scouts of the USA—the top leader in Girl Scouting—resigned. Hundreds of people applied to fill that job.

I didn't.

Leading GSUSA would be far more complex than leading a council. I didn't see myself as having either the skill set or the national clout that the job would require. Girl Scouts almost always hired its top leader from outside—Frances Hesselbein had been the only council CEO ever promoted to lead GSUSA. It was clear that the job would be a headache, because Girl Scouting was starting to face systemic organizational challenges. From my perspective running a successful council in a warm, friendly Southern town, the situation at New York headquarters looked this way: heaven help whoever gets the job.

After eight months, GSUSA announced that it had not filled the job opening. No one who had applied had been hired. A week later Mike and I were on vacation, camping at a music festival in south Texas, when my cell phone rang. It was GSUSA: it was extending the search for a new CEO. And would I please apply.

I called Frances Hesselbein from our pop-up camper in the festival campground.

"Frances, what should I do?"

"You put this phone down right now," Frances said, "and get your résumé together. Your destiny is calling. Girl Scouts needs you."

Mike, who was listening to this exchange, looked at me with an expression like a basset hound. Mike and I often had spent evenings in Nashville watching *Law & Order* on TV, with Mike pointing to the crowded city streets and skyscrapers and saying, "Please don't ever make me go live there!"

There were plenty of good reasons not to apply.

There was one good reason to do it: girls needed leadership.

In our primitive campground, a friend used his battery-powered laptop to hack into our home computer and retrieve my résumé. Mike and I immediately updated it and sent it off to New York City.

That autumn I became CEO of Girl Scouts of the USA. (File this under "Well, you never know": my year and a half of national education grant work at the Kellogg Foundation—which might have looked like a hole in a Girl Scout résumé—turned out to be a big plus with the GSUSA board of directors.)

Imagine a Girl

These parallels between my personal story and the new Girl Scout *Discover, Connect, Take Action* leadership program make me step back and take a broader look at what Girl Scouts can accomplish.

Imagine a girl with no personal success history. No one expects much of her, not even herself. She tries to accomplish something that feels worthwhile to her. She finds out she can do this thing. It gives her confidence to try other things. She keeps trying. She makes mistakes, learns from them, and gains courage to stumble and pick herself up and keep going. She stretches, achieving beyond what others, or even she, thought were her limits. She connects to her world and sees herself as a vital part of it. She makes choices to try to improve not only her own life but also the lives of others. She is gaining character.

This girl, who started out nearly invisible, could one day become the leader of Girl Scouts. She could become:

- President and board chair of the Peter Drucker Foundation.

- Governor of Texas, or prime minister of England or Israel.

- U.S. secretary of state, or senator, or Speaker of the House.

- Worldwide TV personality and billionaire, to whom millions look for advice and compassion.

- Commander of the space shuttle.

- Discoverer of radium, or discoverer of the comet of the millennium.

- Founder of a movement that has touched the lives of 50 million women.

This girl, and thousands upon thousands like her, can find her natural place in a balanced national leadership that makes great decisions and brings us all a better future.

Lady from Savannah

Before I tell you about retooling the Girl Scout movement, let's look at the unlikely way the whole movement started: how 18 girls became 50 million.

At the start of the twentieth century, English military officer and war hero Robert Baden-Powell served in India, Kenya, and other parts of the British Empire. He took an interest in what was then called woodcraft—camping, tracking, and outdoor survival—and wrote books about it, one of which

became a best seller in England and a favorite guide for boys'
groups.

Baden-Powell saw how boys responded to the opportunity
to develop self-reliance, confidence, and personal and leadership
skills. Through his reputation as a war hero and his contacts in
government, Baden-Powell became the leader of the scouting
movement in England. In 1908 he founded the Boy Scouts.[2]

This was an era when girls lived lives of forced inactiv-
ity. Nice girls weren't supposed to run, swim, ride bicycles,
or even raise their arms above their heads. But when girls
saw how much fun the boys were having, they wanted to be
scouts, too. Before the movement was a year old, 6,000 girls
had signed up, using just their initials to avoid detection.
Baden-Powell and the boys thought having girls in their midst
might make them look silly, so in 1910 Baden-Powell's wife
and sister formed Girl Guides in England.[3]

Meanwhile, a well-to-do 50-year-old American widow
from Savannah, Georgia, living in Paris and studying sculp-
ture and occasionally visiting England, chanced to sit beside
Lord Baden-Powell at a luncheon in London. Juliette Gordon
Low was inspired by Baden-Powell's charismatic personality and his work with scouts. In her diary she noted that the
scouting leader saw himself as a servant of his country and
of the scouting movement, and he regarded his own life as
utterly unimportant in the big picture.

----

[2]Boy Scouts of America was formed in 1910.

[3]Girl Guides quickly became the World Association of Girl Guides
and Girl Scouts (WAGGGS), which serves 10 million girls worldwide.
WAGGGS's largest member is the Girl Scouts of the USA.

Thus began a lifelong friendship between Juliette Gordon Low and the Baden-Powell family. It was a crucial moment for Juliette, who realized what Girl Guides could do for girls. Juliette's energy and time suddenly found a purpose. She established a Girl Guide troop in Scotland, then two more in London. In January 1912 she sailed for America carrying a copy of Baden-Powell's *Scouting Manual.*

"Something for the Girls"

On March 12 in Savannah, Juliette called her friends and said, "I have something for the girls of Savannah, and all

America, and we're going to start it tonight." She gathered
18 girls in her house and started the first troop of Girl Scouts
of the USA.

Four years later, 7,000 girls were in Girl Scout troops around
the country, including Hawaii. Four years after that, there were
70,000. By the time Juliette died, in 1927, there were 200,000
Girl Scouts in the United States. Today there are 2.4 million.

Juliette Low used her society contacts, her huge energy,
and her burning desire to open doors for girls to grow the
new Girl Scout movement. When funds fell short, she sold
her pearls to keep the movement strong. Here's a word
picture from her biography, *Lady from Savannah*:

> Perhaps the greatest contradiction of all is that this social
> butterfly and world traveler, flitting restlessly from country
> to country and country house to country house, suddenly
> in middle age threw all her capabilities, driving power, and a
> large part of her financial resources into an effort completely
> foreign to anything she had ever done before, showing a
> tenacity of purpose and an organizing and executive genius
> that those who knew her best had not dreamed she possessed.[4]

If you seek to find the essence of leadership and the
vast potential of girls and women, study the later portion
of Juliette Gordon Low's life. (She died of cancer in 1927,
15 years after founding Girl Scouts.) Imagine Juliette's
verve and her daring when she said, in the 1920 *Girl Scout
Handbook*—a year before the United States amended the

---

[4]Gladys Denny Shultz and Daisy Gordon Lawrence, *Lady from
Savannah* (Philadelphia: Lippincott, 1958; reissued by Girl Scouts
of the USA, 1988).

Constitution to let women vote—"What a jolly, wondrous-working thing a group of girls, all forging ahead together, can be!" See how that revolutionary spirit has inspired, for a whole century, the core values that Juliette instilled in her first 18 girls: service to country, active work and play, self-sufficiency, and the warm power of sisterhood. When you see pictures of Juliette's girls playing basketball in bloomers—unheard-of at the time—you see the spirit that infuses the Girl Scout movement today.

A Place of Our Own

In addition to values of citizenship, service, and active life, Girl Scouts always has provided a sanctuary where girls can be themselves, not bothered or distracted or intimidated by boys. Girls blossom in a unique way in this all-girl environment. It's an opportunity that boys always have taken for granted as their own right. Girls have yearned for the same chance to thrive among their peers; and they do thrive there, in ways beyond what the larger society thinks is possible.

I've seen the truth of this, and been constantly amazed and exhilarated by it, through my quarter-century of Girl Scout leadership. Robert Baden-Powell's choice to make scouting a single-sex experience for both boys and girls showed prescience and did an enormous service for girls.

Emotional reward is not the only value of a single-sex learning environment. One study[5] shows that both girls and

---

[5]A six-year study, published in 2000, by the Australian Council on Educational Research.

boys in single-sex classes score 15 to 22 percent higher on tests than their coeducational peers. I'm not going to agitate for universal single-sex education, but I strongly support the all-girl sanctuary Girl Scouting provides. When girls get together without boys, they feel they're in a safe place to take risks and face challenges. And girls *want* to challenge themselves—which is why 6,000 girls secretly signed up for "boy" scouting in 1908. Girls want to try things they don't know how to do. We've found that to really stretch out and take healthy risks, it helps girls to be in a place where it's okay to fail and recover and try again and again until they succeed.

If you doubt these qualities in girls, go watch a group of young sprites learn the high ropes challenge course at Girl Scout camp. You'll never doubt again.

Learning to Lead

Girl Scouting also gives girls a place where they can learn to lead. At Girl Scouts, we focus on leadership for two reasons. One is, again, that our nation and the world needs the leadership power of girls and women. The other reason is that girls need that same power for themselves. On the personal level, the same qualities that you need to lead well—courage, confidence, character, the ability to communicate, a solid sense of values—are the qualities you need to live well, too.

Here's an example. On a recent visit to a Girl Scout council I met a Girl Scout named Alicia. An accomplished young woman and a devout Catholic, Alicia is a high school senior now; she's been a Girl Scout since she joined Daisy Girl Scouts in kindergarten. Last year the Catholic Committee on

Scouting in her diocese gave Alicia the *Spirit Alive!* Award for her community service. Shortly afterward, she traveled with a group of Girl Scouts to the Caribbean and lived for a week on a tiny island doing marine research on a barrier reef. Alicia's family of modest means never could have afforded her this range of opportunities and skill-building challenges.

Alicia told me that her award and her week of Caribbean hands-on research "each allowed me to pursue one of my passions: devotion to my faith and an interest in marine biology. How many teenagers can boast that they belong to an organization that so seamlessly cultivates such diverse interests?"

I'll go out on a limb and suggest that Alicia is not going to be one of those people that life just sort of happens to. She's going to choose the life she leads. I am humbly grateful to be part of a worldwide movement that has helped her get to this point. Alicia knows who she is, she seems happy, and she's able to focus on things bigger than herself. She will be a powerful asset to the world around her.

Our country needs more girls like that. Millions more. And we can have them.

3 Talk Less, Listen More

If we in the United States want our girls to be confident in themselves and make the most of their inborn potential, we need to wake up to roadblocks we're putting in their way as they try to grow up into their real selves. We're not creating these roadblocks intentionally, and we mean no harm by them. Yet we're advising girls, from a very early age, to embrace a narrow stereotype rather than a wide range of possibilities.

"Boys will be boys, and girls will be girls."

"Sugar and spice and everything nice, that's what little girls are made of."

Ever heard this stereotype? Sure you have. You hear versions of it every day. When you're not hearing it, you're seeing it. Nearly every movie, television program, magazine cover, store window display, or bus stop ad refers in some way to differences between boys and girls. Of course boys and girls *are* different. But we're putting an extra burden on girls when we cross a line from description (here's what we see when we look at girls and boys) to prescription (here's what we *should* see when we look at girls and boys). In our culture today, we step over that line most of the time, and we don't even realize we're doing it.

Here's an example. In 1994 Mike and I were glancing through an FAO Schwartz "ultimate toy" catalog: 60 pages showing happy kids playing with high-end toys. This is

America's premier upscale toy catalog. Professional marketers assembled it through customer research to reflect upscale parents' views of how their kids relate to toys.

Mike and I were shocked at the gender bias we saw in that catalog. We looked closely at how many boys and how many girls appeared in the photos, and whether each child was doing something with the toy (active, in charge) or just watching (passive, not in charge). We knew we were seeing how well-to-do parents view their boys and girls as visible and valuable and able, and as doers, watchers, learners, and decision makers.

Fifty boys were pictured in the catalog, and just 23 girls. Nearly all the boys were pictured in action: riding, throwing, jumping, or wielding a toy. But a third of the girls were just standing around gazing lovingly at a doll or a teddy bear or watching an active boy. The science/technology toy photos showed 10 boys—all of them active—and no girls at all.

Closer inspection revealed one photo of a boy and a girl in a "ball pit" filled with thousands of small plastic balls. Kids could wallow in the pit, toss the balls, and hide among them. In the photo, the girl and the boy were each holding a ball, so both were "active," yet the boy was in the center of the photo, smiling at the camera, while the girl sat at the edge of the photo, smiling at the boy. No photo in the whole catalog showed a girl in charge, front and center, with a boy watching her from the side.

Working with Girl Scouts and observing tens of thousands of children, I've seen that girls and boys are equally hungry to play, and they *all* choose to be active in a front-and-center way with their toys. And girls (young girls, especially) are just as interested as boys are in toys that test and teach what makes the world tick.

Why did FAO Schwartz set up its catalog this way? Did the toy company realize the imbalance? Did it make a business decision to match the parents' view of their kids, no matter how skewed? And if those parents saw their kids as having these limits, then how did the parents' assumptions impact the way their girl children would grow up?

That same year, I read a report examining 20 children's books that had won a prestigious award for excellence. Nineteen of them had no central female character at all. In the one book that did, the central female character was a secretary.

Mike was so moved by the toy catalog and the children's book award that he wrote a song: "See Melanie Run."

See Melanie Run

A six-year-old girl, learning to read
Looks for herself in the pictures
She wants to see what a girl can do
Waves her hand at the teacher
Suddenly, there on the very next page
The smiling face of a girl her age

(continued)

(continued)

See Melanie run!
Run like the wind through this whole wide world
Hey, it's great to be a girl!
See Melanie run!

A twenty-year-old girl, testing her speed
Looks at herself in the mirror
She wants to see what a girl can do
When there's a crowd to cheer her
Goes to the gym with her track shoes on
This year, she'll run the marathon

See Melanie run!
Run like the wind through this whole wide world
Hey, it's great to be a girl!
See Melanie run!

Run like the wind . . .
Run like the wind . . .

A fifty-year-old girl, learning to lead
Looks at herself in the monitor
She wants to see what a girl can do
When she's elected senator
Ready to speak to the crowd outside

Ready to climb clear up to the sky

See Melanie run!
Run like the wind through this whole wide world
Hey, it's great to be a girl!
See Melanie run!

A six-year-old girl, learning to read
Looks for herself in the pictures . . .

Used by permission from Mike Williams © 1995.

Mirror, Mirror

In all forms of media, and in all the ways we express our limited expectations of girls, our society spends way too much time talking at girls rather than listening to them. One of the things we do at Girl Scouts is listen; when you have almost a million caring adult volunteers working with nearly three million girls, you have a lot of conversations going on.

We listen to girls systematically, too. We've been doing that for a long time. Back in 1989 Girl Scouts of the USA commissioned Louis Harris to do a survey—the *Survey on the Beliefs and Moral Values of America's Children*. This was at a time many Americans believed that young people generally held lax values on ambition, drugs, premarital sex, and so on. The common perception was that young people showed little respect and were easy prey to pressure and temptation.

But no one had bothered to ask the kids.

So we did. We asked 5,000 girls and boys across the country how they felt about pressures they faced as adolescents, moral judgments they made in everyday situations, how they viewed their future responsibilities of citizenship, and how adults influenced their moral choices. The kids' answers disproved the gloom-and-doom brigade and said, "We're okay." The reason I'm telling you about this study isn't to celebrate the results; it's to point out that our 1989 Girl Scout research was *the first such study ever done in this country.*

Twenty years later, we followed up on that study (with similarly encouraging results), building on the 1989 findings and asking more specifically about similarities and differences between the moral values of girls and boys. We learned, for example, that girls are more likely than boys to value diversity, give to charity, and volunteer in their communities.

In the year 2000, Girl Scouts of the USA created a whole division at headquarters—the Girl Scout Research Institute (GSRI)—to study girls and try to understand what's going on with them. Here are a few publications from GSRI's first years:

- *Teens before Their Time* (2000). Girls age 8 to 12 talk about challenges and pressures they face.

- *The Girl Difference: Short-Circuiting the Myth of the Technophobic Girl* (2001).

- *The Net Effect: Girls and the New Media* (2002). We studied the Internet habits of girls age 13 to 18.

- *New Directions for Girls Ages 11–17* (2002). Middle and high school girls explore their hopes, fears, and self-images.

- *Feeling Safe: What Girls Say about Emotional and Physical Safety* (2003).

Our Girl Scout research is building Girl Scouting's reputation as the go-to source for information on girls' well-being—though we've only scratched the surface of what we really need to know. We are actively learning, listening, asking girls big questions, and taking their answers seriously.

Let me share with you a few things we've learned.

Beauty and the *Cosmo* Girl

Our culture is good at selling things to girls. One thing we've done a brilliant job of selling them is ideas about what they're supposed to look like: they're supposed to look like the girls you see in movies and on television shows and magazine covers and fashion runways.

That's not what girls generally see when they look in the mirror. They see something else, and they think, "Something is wrong with me." Since they don't look like the *Cosmo* girl, they feel that they are somehow lacking as human beings. Girls' insecurity about appearance is so huge and widespread that even the few girls (and women) who *do* look like the *Cosmo* girl are frequently unhappy with what they see in the mirror. And their unhappiness all too often drives them toward anorexia, destructive personal and sexual relationships, and worse.

In a study called *Beauty Redefined,* the Girl Scout Research Institute asked more than a thousand girls age 13 to 17 about body image. Girls told us they feel negatively affected by the barrage of "here's what a girl is supposed to look like" images they see every day. Nine out of 10 girls said the media or the fashion industry puts "a lot" of pressure on them to be thin. Two-thirds of girls said the image presented by fashion models is too skinny. An equal number said they thought this image is "unrealistic," meaning they themselves expect never to be able to look like that.

Yet a majority of girls admitted they compare their own bodies to what they see in the media, and they sometimes starve themselves or refuse to eat in order to lose weight. Most said they consider fashion "really important." Almost half said fashion magazines give them a body image to strive for.

Girls are confused about their body image. They're confused about how they see themselves and how the world sees them.

We got insight into just how confused in a 2006 GSRI study, *The New Normal? What Girls Say about Healthy Living.* More than 2,000 girls spoke out about unhealthy weight, lack of physical activity, poor eating habits, and how those things tie in with girls' feelings about how their bodies look and how healthy they are. Girls told us they often have a skewed perception of their weight (regardless of how they feel about fashion models). One in three girls age 8 to 17 either thinks she's too heavy when she's actually normal size, or thinks she's normal size when she's actually overweight.

Yet we also found that girls take a more holistic approach to health than boys do. Girls equate being healthy with having good relationships and being social. This creates a strange twist: messages from adults that focus entirely on diet and exercise—"Do this and you'll feel better"—don't work well for a lot of girls, because the girls are thinking of their weight in terms of being accepted. To the girls, healthy living means the absence of harmful behaviors like using drugs, drinking, or smoking; but skipping meals or eating junk food are okay because they're "normal."

Girl Scouting is taking action to help girls clear up their body-image confusion. We've introduced a "healthy media" bill in Congress, which would authorize grants to advance positive images of girls and women in the media, to fund research on the impact of media on girls, and to establish a national task force to improve the way girls and women are portrayed in the media.

To gain traction for this bill, Girl Scouts partnered with the Geena Davis Institute on Gender in the Media, the National Association of Broadcasters, and the National Cable and Telecommunications Association to host a "Healthy Media for Youth" summit in Washington, D.C., in the fall of 2010. We also launched a national public service announcement, produced by the Creative Coalition, called "Watch What You Watch," which helps girls pay attention to media misrepresentations and resist being sexually stereotyped. This public service announcement won a 2011 Gracie Award (named for comedienne and media role model Gracie Allen) for promoting healthy media images for girls and women.

Self-Esteem

A girl's lack of confidence about her body can lead her to make risky choices in terms of her friends, her health, and her sexuality.

Our Girl Scout research shows that the more solid a girl is in her self-esteem, and the more she understands that she has hopeful options in her future, and the more she has a support system to help her keep on a productive path, the less likely she'll be to have sex carelessly or too early (or both) and potentially get pregnant.

Sex isn't the only arena in which low self-esteem can cause girls to do things that limit their future options. A girl's negative feelings about her appearance can easily translate to negative feelings about other aspects of herself, such as intelligence.

The fact that women are underrepresented in almost every field of leadership isn't just because men guard their turf. It's because many women, from an early age, see themselves as not having the capacity to thrive in fields that require sharp minds. When girls opt out of those fields, they often don't feel that they're making a choice; instead they feel they have no choice.

It's not just a matter of girls getting to college and taking a look at the chemical engineering curriculum and deciding, "Hmmm, I think I'll take an easier major." The underlying lack of confidence may go way back before a girl reaches college. If you're 14 and you decide to take general science instead of chemistry, or business math instead of second-year algebra, you are making a life-determining choice that you aren't going to be a scientist or an engineer (or a veterinarian, or a lot of other things). At age 14, you may not realize how these decisions limit the potential you can achieve. Yet by age 14 you already have been influenced for years, by so many facets of our culture, to think that girls in general, and you in particular, never can do X, Y, and Z.

I'm not saying every girl owes it to herself to aim to captain the space shuttle. If a girl understands the choices she's making and has a passion for something that doesn't require math or science, that's fine. But if a girl has brains and aptitude and intellectual curiosity to do more rigorous work, but she shies away from it because she thinks it's uncool to be smarter than the boys—well, Houston, we have a problem.

What We Learn in School

That problem is compounded by what happens to girls in school.

At the Kellogg Foundation, I was program officer for a national series of roundtables with educators and community leaders, hosted by the American Association of University Women (AAUW) in connection with the AAUW study *Shortchanging Girls, Shortchanging America*. These roundtables grappled with evidence that boys saw themselves as rising significantly higher on the professional ladder than girls. If a girl and a boy were equally good at science and math, for instance, Johnny would see himself as the doctor and Sue as the nurse. The hard truth is that Sue saw the same images. What's worse, so did the teachers.

The AAUW research also showed a gender gap in self-esteem that begins early and widens with age. In elementary school, six of 10 girls said, "I'm happy the way I am," but just three in 10 felt that way by the time they got to high school. By contrast, seven of 10 boys liked themselves in elementary school and five of 10 still felt good about themselves in high school.

Further AAUW research showed that teachers were giving girls less praise, less attention, less detailed instruction, and fewer opportunities for learning than they gave boys. And teachers were steering girls away from high-tech, high-paying, highly skilled career fields. (The corruption of gender bias in our country's educational system was soon to be laid bare in shocking detail in Myra and David Sadker's riveting book, *Failing at Fairness: How Our Schools Cheat Girls* [Scribner, 4th ed., 1995].)

I don't want to beat up on teachers, schools, toy companies, book awards, or clothing designers. But the impact of all these messages is disturbingly clear. Do you remember the *South Pacific* song "You've Got to Be Carefully Taught"? That song speaks about how we learn racial bias. The song's point is equally clear about gender bias. American society, in a thousand little ways, carefully teaches boys and girls that girls are inferior, are incapable of excellence, and lack the right stuff to be leaders in any field. Girls therefore expect less of themselves than boys do. They expect that because we all have taught them to.

Friend Me

Girls are really, really good at learning the lessons we teach them. We got a close-up look at just how good they are in a

GSRI study called *Who's That Girl? Image and Social Media.*
We surveyed a thousand girls age 14 to 17 to see how girls
use social media such as Facebook, MySpace, or Twitter. We
weren't just interested in how much girls use those media
(they use them a lot—90 percent use Facebook, 30 percent
use MySpace, and 40 percent have Twitter accounts). We
wanted to find out how girls' use of social media intersects
with their relationships and their self-esteem.

We learned that girls are aware that the stuff they're seeing on those sites—and what they're putting on those sites—
doesn't exactly reflect reality. A big majority of girls surveyed
agreed that "most girls my age use social networking sites to
make themselves look cooler than they really are." Nearly half
said *they* use social networking sites to make themselves look
cooler than they really are.

Most girls told us that when they interact face-to-face,
they come across as smart, kind, and a good influence.
Online, however, they play down those traits and emphasize
coming across as fun, funny, or social. (Girls with low self-
esteem, particularly, are likely to add "sexy" and "crazy" to
that list.) Being smart and kind might be important to girls as
individuals, but they doubt that society at large is looking for,
or appreciates, those qualities. They think society is looking
for the life of the party.

Of course we can't ignore that these are teenagers, a time
of life when people routinely try on personas to see if they fit.
What's the harm in exaggerating a little?

Unfortunately, there's a lot of potential harm. Most girls
we surveyed said they'd had a negative experience on a social
networking site, such as having someone gossip about them

or bully them. Nearly half said social networking often creates jealousy among friends, and they had lost respect for a friend because of something the friend posted on a social network.

Cyber-bullying is no laughing matter. It can cause worse damage than face-to-face bullying because it can spread far faster and broader than word of mouth and never can be deleted. So GSUSA has created an advocacy tool kit that shows Girl Scout councils how to advocate on cyber-bullying issues in their state legislatures.

In 2011 Girl Scouts in Connecticut proposed an amendment to include cyber-bullying in the state's current bullying law. A high school Ambassador Girl Scout named Elizabeth gave eloquent testimony about how she had been bullied, and had been a bully, on the Web. Just as she was about to hit the "send" button on a harmful bullying e-mail about one of her girlfriends, Elizabeth realized the power of the Internet and decided she didn't want to hurt her friend that way. She turned the potential crisis into an opportunity by coming forward to speak for the amendment.

It isn't just girls' high school social life that can be hurt via the social media. Girls are aware that things they post on networking sites may sooner or later make them miss a job opportunity, keep them from being accepted into a college, get them in trouble with their teachers or parents, or cause others to lose respect for them. But they post on those sites anyway because they want to be liked. They want to be what they feel they're expected to be.

Which, as we've seen, isn't exactly what and who they are. And in many cases it's not really who they want to be. So in spite of the short-term rewards of thinking "I'm liked" or "I'm cool," the social network mask that girls wear can be confusing as well as potentially damaging.

Part of our job at Girl Scouts—part of everyone's job who cares about even one girl—is to help girls develop a solid core of self-knowledge and values that will guide each girl through the confusion of growing up and make her better able to understand who she really is, what she's really capable of achieving, and who she really wants to be.

Leadership

As we talk about self-esteem and confusion, it's not fair to present girls as shrinking violets or delicate creatures who easily can be crushed. In fact, the opposite is true. The fact that some girls do rise above centuries of high walls, low ceilings, and closed doors is proof that many girls are strong, resilient, and smart. Girls also are caring and sincerely interested in the greater good. My point in this book is that all of us, if we care about lending a hand to fix what's ailing the United States, need to see that we haven't yet done all we can to bring out girls' strengths. As a result, we all are suffering a lack of leadership benefits that girls can provide *for us* if we'll take the lid off and turn girls' abilities loose to flourish.

Girl Scouts found encouraging evidence of girls' abilities, and disturbing news about how our culture's "keep the lid on" is blocking the flourishing, in a major GSRI study, *Change It Up! What Girls Think about Leadership.* This nationwide survey of what girls think about leadership, and how girls' opinions differ from boys', found that after age 10, girls' confidence in their own leadership ability begins a long, slow decline due to the combination of influences I've been talking about.

We need to reverse these influences. Leadership isn't just about corner offices. It's about confidence and integrity in your own life, and knowing who you are and what's important to you and your community, regardless of what title you hold. Girl Scouting's goal is not that every girl must be a top executive. Our goal is to help every girl set her own personal goals high, believe that she can meet them, and live her life with purpose.

Yet our task must go way beyond just saying, "You go, girl!" We also have to show girls that there's a place for the kind of leader that girls believe they can be.

A Different Approach

The *Change It Up!* study showed that one reason girls may not strive toward positions of leadership is because girls don't aspire to lead in traditional male command-and-control style. Instead girls have another leadership model in mind. *Change It Up!* reveals that girls have very definite ideas of what their own leadership style can be, but it's not a style that our overall culture celebrates—yet. Girls don't yet think the world wants the kind of leadership they can contribute.

What kind is that? *Change It Up!*, which surveyed both boys and girls, showed that girls are much more likely to define leadership as standing up for values and beliefs, bringing people together to get things done, and trying to change the world for the better. Boys were more likely to say that they want to be their own boss, that they want more power, that they like being in charge, and that being in a position of leadership will help them make more money.

Boys' view of leadership is what we've taught them to aspire to. A boy's path to success is clear. Be a leader. Stand out in the crowd. Take charge.

A girl's path is not so clear. Be confident, yes—but don't get too far ahead of the boys or they'll think you're bossy. You won't be liked, and you might even make people mad.

What's amazing and encouraging to me is that girls, in spite of how our culture has taught them not to aspire to feel that "I can be a leader," still have a positive concept of a leadership style that is different from command and control. It's more cooperative, more inclusive, more eager to listen to the opinions of others, and more willing to seek the strengths of others. And in spite of the fact that girls receive little encouragement for this view of leadership, and in spite of limited space for it at the national table, the girls we've surveyed agree that their style of leadership is a viable, positive way to Get Things Done.

Boys and girls both set the bar pretty high when it comes to what it takes to be a leader, including the ability to be assertive, confident, and persuasive in addition to honest, creative, and caring. But boys, more than girls, feel that "I can do that." Of the girls we surveyed, nearly all think anyone should be able to learn the skills it takes to be a leader; but just one girl in five believes she already possesses those skills.

I emphasize again the disconnect between who girls think they are and who we try to make them be. A big factor in that disconnect is that we haven't listened enough to girls. In Girl Scout research, girls are saying loud and clear that they want to have an impact. They want to make a difference. They want to be strong. They want to learn and problem-solve in collaborative, safe environments. They want to learn by doing.

What is it we're afraid we'll lose, if we give them a chance?

A Personal Adviser

A few years ago I was given an oversize Girl Scout Groovy Girl doll, a prototype for a licensing agreement we formed with the Manhattan Toy Company. Groovy Girls are multicultural and celebrate individuality and friendship. Girl Scouting is energized to put a product out into the marketplace that is both girl-positive and cool.

That Groovy Girl is my personal adviser. I keep her in a chair close to my desk (by a window where she gets a view of the Empire State Building), and sometimes I'll go over and sit with her and ask her what we should do next.

That doll reminds me to focus on what's really important. She reminds me what girls need. She tells me, "You can sit around all day and come up with ways to teach girls and train them, but in the end, what's really best is to allow girls to speak, and make sure people really hear them."

Girl Scouting—and all of America—has a real opportunity to raise girls who can make our world a better place. If we listen to girls, we'll clearly hear them telling us that this is what they already want to do. And they will do it if only everyone quits getting in their way.

4 A Logical Conclusion

s women's style of leadership more effective than men's? Should men step aside and give women a turn?

That's a trick question, because it isn't an either-or choice. There's increasing evidence that men and women working together provide the best leadership and decision making. What we need is a blended balance.

To achieve that blended balance, we first have to realize that leadership today is *out* of balance. Our culture still sees leadership from a masculine point of view. We talk about whether a person is decisive enough or authoritative enough to be a leader. We equate charisma with ego and dominance more than with empathy and compassion. We think if you're too compassionate, you're probably not a strong leader.

Women who rise to the top in business or politics often feel they have to cultivate a male point of view or behave like men to be taken seriously. But when women do lead in a traditional male command-and-control way, the response is more likely the "b" word than "Atta girl!"

Women need to own part of this imbalance. We haven't been good enough at valuing our unique strengths. We haven't encouraged our nation or our communities to celebrate the way women see the world. We need to do that a lot better if we're ever to approach parity. In 2007, among United Nations member nations the United States ranked

67th in women's participation in national legislature, behind
Cuba and Afghanistan.[1] The 2010 midterm elections installed
17 percent women in Congress. While the visibility of high-
profile politicians such as Nancy Pelosi, Hillary Clinton, and
Sarah Palin may make it look like females have their hands
all over politics, the number of women in Congress today is
actually lower than in 1979. These numbers have nothing to
do with women's leadership potential. They have everything
to do with the fact that voters—including women—aren't
yet convinced that women's style of leadership can solve our
national challenges.

A New Majority

The recession of 2008 has trampled jobs in traditionally male
fields like construction and manufacturing. In 2010, for the first
time, women became a majority in the workplace. Yet they're
still a small minority in executive offices and boardrooms.

*The White House Project Report: Benchmarking Women's
Leadership*, published in 2009, reviewed women's participation
in 10 job sectors in our country: academia, business, journal-
ism, film and television, law, the military, nonprofits, politics,
religion, and sports. On average, across those 10 sectors, women
hold just 18 percent of leadership positions (they're highest in
academia, and fewest in the military). Yet more women than
men are earning college degrees. And in all sectors except the
military, women are at least half of the staff or line workers.

Marie Wilson, founder and president of the White House
Project, the organization that prepared *The White House Project*

---

[1]United Nations compilation of data from member states, 2008.

Report, talks about the importance of reaching "critical mass." This nuclear physics term refers to the amount of something needed to start a chain reaction—an event that leads irreversibly to a new situation. By critical mass, Wilson means arriving at a point where women leaders are evaluated first for their abilities rather than for the anomaly of being female.

Wilson uses the example of the Supreme Court. One woman on the court is newsworthy because she's a first. If we have two, women are still an exception. But when we reach three out of nine—as the court currently stands—it stops being unusual. The nominee for the next vacancy likely won't be evaluated on the basis of gender but on her or his worthiness to make important and sometimes momentous decisions.

Critical mass for women in many other leadership arenas will take time to reach. Consider the Wimbledon Championships, the flagship of tennis tournaments. The first match was played in 1877, and the women's competition began in 1884. One hundred and twenty-three years later, in 2007, Wimbledon finally started paying equal prizes to the male and female winners. That year the chairman of the All England Lawn Tennis and Croquet Club, Tim Phillips, said that the time was right to bring the subject "to a logical conclusion."

In terms of the book you are reading, critical mass for women's leadership will arrive on the day when you can put this book aside and wonder, "What was Kathy so worked up about?"

The Norway Experiment

The government of Norway arrived at a logical conclusion in 2003 when it enacted legislation requiring that women hold at least 40 percent of board seats in publicly traded Norwegian companies. Iceland and Spain have since followed suit with quotas of their own. The thinking in Norway is that it makes sense to use all of the nation's human capital, rather than just the male half of it.

This idea came not from a social liberal but from conservative businessman Audun Lysbakken, who at the time was Norway's minister of children, equality, and social inclusion. Lysbakken told a global roundtable on board diversity in 2010 that gender equity was both a prerequisite and a key factor for economic growth. "If we neglect the need to empower women, we pay for that neglect by weakening our countries' economic performance."

Quotas for women, imposed by legislation or any other source, don't sit easy with me. I think women's unique strengths deserve a place at the table on their own merits. Still, it's worth looking at the result of Norway's experiment, and at startling results from other situations where women have provided balance in leadership. What does Norway's economy look like? In mid-2010, *Newsweek* named Norway "the only Western industrialized state to escape the global economic meltdown relatively unscathed. It boasts a healthy banking sector, record-low unemployment, and one of the hottest sovereign wealth funds around."

No one can say just how much of Norway's financial success is due to women on corporate boards. But neither is anyone pointing to other factors as exclusive keys. And many voices are questioning whether more women in roles of leadership worldwide might have prevented the 2008 economic meltdown.

Sally Helgesen and Julie Johnson devote a whole chapter to the subject in their book *The Female Vision: Women's Real Power at Work* (Berrett-Koehler, 2010). As Helgesen and Johnson explain it, women in general are more likely to be cautious, while men are more apt to be competitive and go all in.

Women working in the financial sector at the time of the 2008 collapse were mostly playing second string; they weren't senior enough to make the big decisions or place the large bets that ended up backfiring. There wasn't a balanced vision in place to temper competitiveness with caution, and we all ended up losing.

As a side note to Norway's success, it's worth mentioning that women in the United States currently make up only 15 percent of the total of corporate board directors, and many corporations have either token female board presence or none at all. Those male bastions may be making a huge error. A recent study of the Fortune 500 shows that American corporations whose boards are at least one-quarter women outperform companies with the smallest level of female board participation by 53 percent on return on equity, by 42 percent on return on sales, and by 66 percent on return on invested capital.[2]

Being Yourself

Some women who do reach high levels of authority and influence decide not to stay, because the experience of being there grates against their values. Many find it hard to move into

---

[2]Catalyst/Chubb Corporation, 2007.

roles of leadership and still be authentic to their self-image and to the inherently feminine qualities they possess.

Authenticity—a quality that women strive to nurture in themselves and that they're loath to sacrifice—can be hard to hang on to when few around you are thinking like you or looking like you. If you value long-term payoffs, collaboration, and working for the greater good, it can be hard to put those values out front when others around you are focused on competition, individual gain, and short-term gratification.

Helgesen and Johnson interviewed women who either had left high positions or were considering doing so. One phrase kept coming up: "I decided it just wasn't worth it." It wasn't that the women didn't want to work hard or be thrillingly involved in their work. It was that they didn't relate to their companies' traditional reward systems.

A subsequent study showed that in general, men put a higher value on benefits and compensation than women do. Paychecks are a man's way to keep score. For women, the paycheck is less about competition and more about means to an end such as taking care of themselves and their families. When women speak of things they value, high on the list are the quality of the relationships with others on the job, and the chance to contribute to a larger purpose.

That's exactly what girls told us in our own GSRI research.

When women find that traditional rewards of leadership don't line up with their values, they may head for the door. And who can blame them? It's fruitless to say, "You should stick it out, right or wrong." Women—especially strong, confident women—rightfully value quality of life, day by day, and they feel it's okay to seek a place where they can surround themselves with people they relate to and opportunities to accomplish good work without the requirement to "man up" and compete.

(Maybe this is one reason that women—some of whom have left the big-company corporate arena—have become the large majority of owners of small businesses in this country.)

For women to reach critical mass in leadership, we have to find a way to keep them actually in the system. What can we do, in our culture and in our workplaces, to make leadership opportunities more accessible and more attractive so women can arrive and stay there to achieve the goal of blended leadership?

It's going to take women of corporate and political success giving each other better support, and opening truly collaborative dialogue with male coworkers. It's going to take building a culture that values both women's and men's ways of approaching work, and that gains strength by integrating the two. It's going to take women and men seeking answers together, not just women struggling toward the top.

Support (or Not) in the Workplace

I've personally been fortunate in finding support. When I became CEO of the Girl Scout council in middle Tennessee, an informal group of nonprofit female leaders in Nashville took me under their wing. The Margarita Sisters' hallmark was a cooperative, nurturing spirit. We met once a month for 10 years. They still meet regularly and I keep in touch by e-mail. We completely trust each other and can speak openly about any struggle. If one of us has a problem, the others show up to help. Today I still reach back to that group often as a source of sharing and perspective.

Many women leaders may not easily find that kind of support. Studies have shown again and again that women in the workplace receive less mentoring than men—not because women tend not to *be* mentors, but because the men who hold the majority of top positions tend to mentor other men. When women are undermentored, it's not just the secret club handshakes that they miss out on. They may not get access to practical leadership lessons. They may have a hard time building networking relationships that men already have in place. And should an aspiring young woman look toward the top and see only men there, those men, even if they mentor her, may not choose, or know how, to nurture her uniquely feminine ways of viewing the world and the contributions that those feminine views can make toward the corporate bottom (and top) line.

Not only does our culture undervalue the leadership traits that women bring to the table, but we also fail to support women who already are in leadership. That's not only about depriving women of chances to network or be mentored or, for that matter, denying them equal pay. It's also about how our public eye scrutinizes women in unfair ways.

Envision two top leaders, a man and a woman, who each appear in a public leadership moment. Which one do you think will be subject to more comments about weight, body shape, haircut, attire, and tone of voice? And which leader will generate more discussion about the content of his or her corporate or political message?

When Hillary Clinton attended the United Nations in New York in autumn 2010, a good bit of news coverage focused on a hair clip she wore that some people thought was too informal. I don't know which irritates me more: the news space that media devote to this sort of trivia, versus reporting on the worth of the work, or the implication that the public is more interested in hairpins than international diplomacy.

When Sarah Palin became a candidate for vice president, much was made of her physical attractiveness (some called her "Caribou Barbie"). When Elena Kagan presented herself to the Supreme Court as the first female solicitor general, there was a fair amount of discussion of what she wore. And in 2005, when then Secretary of State Condoleezza Rice wore a skirt and heeled boots to visit the Wiesbaden Army Airfield, those boots apparently represented sex and power—some actually threw around the word *dominatrix*.

Another way we treat male and female leaders differently is in terms of family responsibility. During the 2008 presidential campaign, Sarah Palin's ability to balance a high-profile political career with parenting her five children was a hot topic. Some questioned whether she'd be able to devote full attention to the job. Meanwhile no one was doubting congress*men*'s abilities to fulfill their jobs while parenting.

It is fair to say that women generally bear more hands-on care of their families than men do. More and more men are taking on these responsibilities, but in most cases, women still run the house. In that respect, women who seek an active role in leadership may indeed have more on their plate than men do. This doesn't just affect women who already are in places of leadership; it impacts the rise of women who are on their way there. Men are typically encouraged to put their entire focus on work, or at least split their attention 75 percent work and 25 percent home. But women get criticized for even a 60/40 split. Women of means may be able to hire nannies, cooks, and maids to absorb minute-to-minute homemaking. But the majority of working American women have their hands full making enough money to keep things going and create a good life for their kids. How are those women supposed to compete with somebody who isn't carrying that burden? The choice, for a woman, often seems to be either-or. It may not seem doable to achieve both tasks.

Mothers now are the primary breadwinners or co-breadwinners in almost two-thirds of American families.[3] That's a big change in recent years. In 1967, women were only a third of all workers. Women today are playing by new rules. And child care, household responsibilities, family and medical leave, and flexible work schedules have become a big part of the conversation in corporations and in politics.

Some companies have come up with innovative ways to help. The accounting and consulting firm Deloitte, for example, has implemented an effort called Mass Career Customization. Based on a corporate lattice rather than a corporate ladder, it allows employees of either gender to increase or scale back responsibilities on a periodic basis, depending on what else is happening in their lives.

In 1993, Norway instituted a paternal quota for paid time off after a child is born. That time has increased, over

---

[3] *The Shriver Report: A Woman's Nation Changes Everything*, by Maria Shriver and the Center for American Progress, 2009.

the years, and now stands at 10 weeks (though some urge to make it 14). Does this time off hurt the bottom line? Audun Lysbakken compares his country's gross domestic product to that of the United States, noting that on a per capita basis Norway's is 20 percent higher. That advantage, he told the UN Commission on the Status of Women, has more to do with Norway having "sound family and gender policies, as part of a sound economic policy" than it does with oil production. Lysbakken says the greatest gains countries can achieve economically and politically come by empowering women, ensuring equal opportunity, health care, and increasing women's active participation in paid working life.

In a woman-supportive workplace environment, men more equitably share the role of child care, and the national economy and culture encourage them to do so through both approval and more tangible benefits. In such an economy, not only can women better focus on building leadership skills, but they also aren't penalized disproportionately for gaps of experience and opportunity that arise while taking time off to have children.

If you change the workplace and the cultural environment to offer greater flexibility and balance to both genders in their family roles, as Norway has done, the economic playing field levels out, to the benefit of us all—including the welfare of our children.

Making Impressions

In early 2011 as Susana Martinez was preparing to be sworn in as the country's first Hispanic woman governor (of New Mexico), she told a *Los Angeles Times* reporter that in striving to be elected to the office she had focused more on the challenge of fulfilling the requirements of the job than on blazing a trail for young Latina girls who might follow her.

I understand Governor Martinez's focus, and I celebrate her success and the role modeling that she now is providing for Latina girls. Her statement reminds us, though, that young people are watching us as we face our own leadership challenges. The ways we act, and the values we put into action, send strong messages to youth who are just entering a world of responsibility and opportunity.

We make impressions without even trying. But what might we accomplish for young people if we *were* trying? At a recent dinner to welcome the first executive director of UN Women (a new department at the United Nations dedicated to improving the status of women worldwide), I shared a table with the honoree, Michele Bachelet, former president of Chile. In our dinner conversation she talked about how rarely women in unusual leadership roles will acknowledge the fact that it was challenging, as a woman, to reach and perform that job.

She said, "We need to be willing to talk, as women, about how different it was to be in our roles in a predominately male culture or arena. The more we share that female experience with each other and with our daughters, the more likely it is for girls to start believing that they can follow in our path and learn from our experience and achieve similar success."

So: what would actually happen if we worked intentionally to instill self-esteem and confidence in girls, so once they reached doorways to leadership, they wouldn't be restricted by the boxes that society tries to put them in? What if women who move into top leadership roles made a point of sharing with others their authentic feelings about what it's like to break barriers in a mainly male field? What if those ground-breakers went out of their way to help girls feel that it's not only an exceptional woman who can achieve success? What if women leaders made it part of their job to tell girls that the feminine leadership style, though it's different from the traditional model of men, can accomplish great things?

And what if, once women do take a first step into leadership, we all nurture and buoy them so they can maintain their resilience no matter what the world brings next? Here's a story about how that can work. Girl Scouting has a national program called Camp CEO. We pair aspiring high school business leaders with high-ranking corporate women, in a sleeves-rolled-up camp mentoring session. Girl Scouts' national board chair, Connie Lindsey, who is not at all a camper, put on her T-shirt and shorts and bug spray to spend a week talking in an open, truthful, informal setting about her journey from childhood in public housing to becoming the senior vice president and highest-ranking African American woman at Northern Trust. She delighted in sharing her uniquely feminine approach to leadership, and how she has nurtured it in a predominately male banking culture. Girls hungered to hear her stories. Connie treated the girls as protégés. Several of them, years later, are staying in touch with her as they cling to their values while rising in the marketplace.

It's a wonderful thing to see Connie and hundreds of other executive women who are former Girl Scouts, partnering with girls in Camp CEOs all across the country, sharing their stories and demystifying their journeys to the top of the corporate ladder.

I want to finish this chapter with one more tale about women helping women be leaders. It's about a world record from the sport of college basketball. Perhaps you recall the names of some of college basketball's famous players over the years, such as LeBron James, Michael Jordan, Kobe Bryant, Magic Johnson, and Larry Bird.

Here's a factoid for you to ponder. The all-time collegiate record for consecutive basketball wins—89 games over a three-year stretch—belongs to the 2010 University of Connecticut *women's* team. Yet on that team of great athletes, you may not know a single player's name. The press coverage of the UConn women's amazing run focused not on individual heroics but on the value that the players placed on working together.

Eighty-nine wins in a row by the team. It has set a leadership mark for every player and every fan in the entire history of basketball. And it was done by girls.

5 Facing the Brutal Truths

After Girl Scouts of the USA hired me as CEO, they gave me three months to wind things up with the council in Nashville. One night during this period, Mike and I went to a local Mexican restaurant to eat enchiladas and catch up on each other's activities. After the waiter took our order, I told Mike, "Headquarters in New York called. The public relations people are asking what my top three priorities are going to be as new CEO."

Mike is an author as well as a musician, and he has great belief in the power of brevity. "Let's see if you can express each priority in a simple sentence," he said. "And of course one word in each priority will be 'girl.'"

We were honing in on essentials right away. No matter what your job description is in Girl Scouting, your real focus always has to be on girls, because girls are the reason Girl Scouting exists. My plate was going to be full at GSUSA, but the point of it all was to do great things for millions of girls. So instead of responding to the PR request by talking about managing a $60 million operational budget or supervising 500 headquarters staff or coordinating services with more than 300 Girl Scout councils all over the country, Mike and I started talking about helping girls.

Early in the conversation, I mused, "You know, people are going to look to me to be the voice for girls."

Mike snagged a pen from a waiter, and wrote on a napkin:

Be the voice for girls.

"Okay," he said. "That's one."

We talked about the impact Girl Scouting has on girls. "It's way more than camp and cookies and singing songs while roasting marshmallows," I said. "It's more about inspiring girls to dig deep into their own possibilities, so they can figure out how to lead good and productive lives."

On the napkin, Mike wrote:

Find the leader in each girl.

He looked at me and grinned. "Hey, if we get one more five-syllable line, we'll have a haiku.[1] And of course one of the words has to be 'girl.'"

We played around with Girl Scout slogans like "Where girls grow strong" and "For every girl, everywhere." As we juggled buzzwords and tried new combinations, we suddenly looked at each other and said in almost the same breath:

Help each girl stand tall.

As a Christmas gift, Mike's mother cross-stitched our priority haiku for us. It hangs behind my desk at Girl Scout headquarters. It reminds me why we all come to work each day.

---

[1]Haiku is an ancient Japanese form of poetry. A haiku has three lines: five syllables in the first line, seven in the second, and five in the third. It's a fine challenge to say something worthwhile in 17 syllables.

Time for Change

I began as CEO of Girl Scouts of the USA in November 2003. Two months later we were deciding to reinvent the entire Girl Scout movement. Two months after that, at Girl Scouts' triennial meeting of council CEOs and board chairs, 700 top Girl Scout staff and volunteers from all over the country were chanting in unison, *The status quo has got to go!*

At that point, no one was saying the Girl Scout movement was in crisis. We weren't falling apart. We weren't broke. We were a stable American icon with a brand known everywhere and traditional values rooted in family, community, and nation. Nearly three million girls enjoyed Girl Scouts each year.

Yet Girl Scouting was in a condition that, if a few more years passed without change, we might find ourselves regretfully saying as the doors closed for the last time, "The handwriting was on the wall. We just didn't see it."

What does a company look like when it's starting to enter that condition?

The scary thing is, it looks perfectly normal. Business is loping along. There's no drama. What has always worked is still working fairly well. The machine is oiled and widgets are popping out. Maybe sales have slowed a little, but people tell each other to relax: It's just a slight downtrend. No need to panic. We'll recover soon; let's just keep doing what we do. Maybe tighten our belts a little. Trim some fat. Nothing drastic. Really, we're fine.

Later, you look back and see that the world was passing the company by. What it needed right then was not belt-tightening but major surgery.

When a company slips into this kind of crisis, no one is expecting it or is even willing to consider the possibility that it's happening. People blame the warning signs on things that are relatively easy to deal with. They convince themselves that what worked before will work again: "Don't fix what ain't broke."

I'm not talking about companies that don't care. This kind of crisis doesn't happen just to companies whose motto is "Acme Widgets: we're no worse than anybody else." It also happens in companies that have prospered through great ideas, hard work, and good people.

It happened to Woolworth's. It happened to U.S. Steel. It happened to Kmart. It happened to Pan American and Eastern Airlines and Trans World Airlines. It happened to the whole Swiss watch industry. It has happened to hundreds of organizations, and it very easily could have happened to us.

When Girl Scouts of the USA began to confront its challenges in 2004, we were already facing membership decline. Historically, the traditional way for girls to take part in Girl Scouting was by joining a troop. But troop membership had begun shrinking in the early 1990s, partly because girls, especially as they aged into middle school, were starting to feel that belonging to a troop was uncool.

To keep membership numbers up, and to put into action a GSUSA slogan that scouting is "For Every Girl, Everywhere," Girl Scout councils started to offer nontroop outreach activities: short-term, specialized programs that often took place over two or three days or even on a single afternoon. These interesting, attractive events did serve a diverse range of girls. But the activities often had to be delivered by staff instead of volunteers, which was more expensive. And outreach girls might experience only a few days of activities in a year, compared to weekly troop programs that continued through the school year.

So we were bolstering our membership at a higher per-girl cost, and giving these added members a briefer and less comprehensive program. This experiment was bold and innovative, and it was worth trying, but it wasn't a sustainable long-term way to deliver Girl Scouting. And with more than 300 Girl Scout councils each struggling to maintain girl membership and invent new activities to attract girls, the overall movement was losing its sense of exactly what it was that we deliver to girls. We couldn't tell the world exactly what a girl experienced in Girl Scouting, nor could we show, in tangible detail, how she benefited from it.

Girl Scouting could have kept going, slowly declining, for many more years. But in a world growing more complex, we were becoming just another option in a sea of choices for girls. We were losing the ability to see ourselves—and for the world to see us—as a primary place for girls to participate, learn, experience, and grow in essential ways.

During my years in Girl Scout councils, I had been aware of these developments, and the problems seemed serious but didn't feel really urgent. However, shortly after I became CEO of GSUSA, I got a rude awakening when I made a visit to Australia and did some research on Girl Guides in Canada. Our movement in those countries had seriously diminished, and the same could happen to Girl Scouts in the United States. I saw that if we didn't change in a big way, we were heading toward a decline from which there could be no recovery.

Brutal Truths

The week I arrived in New York, someone gave me a book called *Reinventing Strategy* by management expert Willie Pietersen (John Wiley & Sons, 2002). I eagerly read this how-to manual for putting into practice the management philosophy of Jim Collins's groundbreaking *Good to Great* (HarperCollins, 2001)—a book I had devoured earlier along with the works of Peter Drucker, Tom Peters, Meg Wheatley, and Peter Senge. Willie Pietersen's book convinced me that Girl Scouts needed to rethink our core purpose: the basis of who we are and what we are about. It also convinced me that Girl Scouting had the strength and the public support to survive comprehensive reexamination and to emerge as the world's best girl-serving agency.

Pietersen's book also affirmed something I already knew: change from the top down is not nearly as powerful, and does not sustain and thrive as well, as change by engagement from the bottom up. So as 2004 dawned and GSUSA's board of directors and I opened the door to major transformation, we knew we'd need support and agreement from all Girl Scout councils, from our one million volunteers, and, of course, from America's girls.

How do you engage that grassroots support? You go to them and ask their opinions. You listen to their answers. You let them know you are hearing them. You trust that the ones in the trenches can bring great energy and creative thinking to the service of girls.

We assembled a strategy team of 26 top volunteers and staff from GSUSA headquarters and from Girl Scout councils. This team's first task was to make a case for change: to present, to everyone in Girl Scouting, a reality check that could motivate innovative thinking to bust through roadblocks. Our strategy team rolled up its sleeves to discover what Jim Collins calls "brutal truths" that confront the organization.

Brutal is the right word. When you're taking an honest look at what is wrong with an organization, it can be painful. This particularly is true in the nonprofit sector, where services are delivered largely by volunteers whose passion for the cause, rather than a paycheck, is what attracts their time and energy. Facing brutal truths can weaken that passion. It's tempting instead to avoid thinking about and confronting problems, so nobody will get upset and leave. It's easy for nonprofits to develop a culture of niceness that prevents people from telling the truth about how things really are. But once we started digging into our own realities, it became impossible for any of us to keep smiling and saying everything was all right.

We Brought to Light These Brutal Truths:

- Our cherished traditions of Girl Scouting—a longtime source of strength and bonding for our volunteers and girls—were keeping us from being flexible enough to respond quickly to the way the world was changing around us. Adult volunteers were craving the same warm and fuzzy feelings from Girl Scouting that they got when they were children. Our movement was being pushed by the past instead of pulled by the future.

- The United States' demographics were changing, and Girl Scouts' image and our membership weren't keeping up with the changes. For example, Hispanics in our country increased by more than half in the last decade of the twentieth century, becoming a larger minority than African Americans. How was Girl Scouting seen by first-generation Latino families, who had no built-in history and tradition with our program? Girl Scouting always has tried to reach all girls—we started having racially integrated Girl Scout troops in 1917—so we needed to find out how Latina girls, and girls of every other culture, felt about us and what they needed in their own lives so we could be relevant to them.

- We couldn't coherently answer, "What is the Girl Scout experience?" Our program had diffused throughout the country to the point where any girl's scouting experience might have little in common with the experience of a sister Girl Scout. This meant we couldn't tell families, donors, and legislators, "Here is the measurable benefit that each girl gets from her time in scouting."

- We were a group of adults trying to define what girls wanted, and we were doing it from the outmoded perspective of how the world had been when we were girls. We were talking to (rather than listening to) girls whose world was different. What we were saying to them wasn't resonating in their reality.

- Girl-adult partnerships always had been a core principle of Girl Scouting. Yet in practice we had lapsed into seeing youth as passive participants to be served, not as active agents to design their own service. Research clearly showed us that if strong relationships are fostered between the generations, results can be transformative, because kids are eager to stretch, act boldly, learn, and step out in leadership roles when adults are encouraging and supporting them. Yet Girl Scout volunteers often sought to save time and energy by just running the group rather than helping the girls run it themselves. Also, GSUSA wasn't giving council volunteers enough support or training to help them engage their troops in true partnership.

Our Program Delivery Was Fragmented

Eileen Doyle, GSUSA's vice president of program, has a bookcase in her office crammed with a mismatched, disorganized mess of books, activity guides, and manuals that we were using in various Girl Scout programs as we began the transformation process. The pile looks like it could topple at any moment.

Eileen says, "It's a nice visual: it holds a little bit of every-thing, and as a result, there's no unifying theme; it ends up representing nothing at all. All around the country, the Girl Scout experience depended on which little booklet you had or didn't have, whether it was a national manual or guidebook or something a troop or council had put together by itself or in cooperation with a regional or local partner. Girls were taking part in a myriad of different activities, and nobody around the country could consistently say, 'Girl Scouts is about *this*.' If you happened to be in this troop, it was about arts and crafts. If you were in this one, it was science and robotics. A third troop might have different things entirely."

Our Girl Scout program wasn't taking full advantage of past skills learned and milestones achieved to create a girl's overall success journey in scouting. Except for earning individual patches and achieving Girl Scouts' top honors (the Gold, Silver, and Bronze Awards), girls didn't see themselves making systematic progress toward some rewarding goal.

In his book *Strategic Learning* (John Wiley & Sons, 2010), Willie Pietersen tells a story about the importance of focus. He and his wife planted geraniums every spring in their New York apartment window boxes. Willie's wife's plants were lush and healthy; Willie's were scrawny. It drove Willie crazy until she told him her secret: she would ruthlessly use her scis-sors to behead spent flowers and prune weaker stems. That way, the plants could concentrate on growing new flowers from the remaining healthy stems.

"The geranium analogy," Willie says, "applies to every living system, whether a garden or a business. Whenever you remove the underperforming parts of any system, all the life forces of that system become concentrated on the few things that matter most, and that system will flourish."

An organization that lets its underperforming parts continue, that doesn't prune to concentrate its efforts on what's growing best, will end up as scrawny as Willie's geraniums. That's pretty much the condition that Girl Scouts' program for girls found itself in: in spite of the heartfelt ways that councils planned events and volunteers and staff delivered them, the program experience for girls was overgrown and needed pruning.

Our Organizational System Needed Restructuring

Girl Scouting is what's known as a federated nonprofit. The national organization, Girl Scouts of the USA, sets broad policy and provides overall direction, programs, activity resource materials, some fund-raising coordination, and management counseling to Girl Scout councils.

The councils—whose jurisdictions are like a jigsaw puzzle covering the whole United States—are each a separate 501(c)(3) nonprofit corporation[2] that delivers the program and services to girls. Councils organize troops for girls, recruit girl and volunteer members, do their own fund-raising, develop

[2]501(c)(3) is the Internal Revenue Code section that sets out the rules these organizations have to follow to be tax-exempt.

their own community relations, and own and run their own campgrounds, recreational facilities, and business offices.

In 2004 each of our 312 independent councils was accustomed to running itself with what they often felt was inadequate support from the home office. Not only was it hard to say what the Girl Scout experience was for any individual girl, but it also was hard to say exactly what a council was supposed to be. Big councils might serve 60,000 girls. The smallest served fewer than a thousand. Council annual budgets ranged as high as $10 million, but nearly a hundred councils had operating budgets below $1 million, meaning they couldn't provide staffing and infrastructure to deliver a top-notch program for girls.

Our Traditional Funding Model Wasn't Sufficient

The financial strength of Girl Scouting was originally built on the entrepreneurial skills of women at a time when they didn't have positions of corporate leadership and they weren't able to exert power in family finances. To fund the movement, these women created three internal revenue streams: the cookie sale, which is the most successful marketing and funding model in U.S. nonprofits; girl and adult membership dues; and sales of Girl Scout merchandise (uniforms, manuals, badges).

These internal revenue streams have grown Girl Scouting well, in the decades since Juliette Low's time. But they aren't sufficient for our future growth. And it's risky to put so many eggs in so few baskets. Girl Scouting now needs to generate contributions from corporate, public, and private sources. Councils have sought such contributions with limited success. And GSUSA has raised revenue through national partnerships with corporations, such as the sale of Dairy Queen Thin Mint

Blizzards and Manhattan Toy Company Girl Scout Groovy Girls. But private or corporate donors have a sensible habit of wanting to see specific results for their dollars. They want measurable outcomes, something they can point to and say, "Our gift achieves this." Platitudes and ethereal concepts such as "Well, you'll be helping girls" don't open the vault.

In 2004, Girl Scouting wasn't able to come up with answers to suit donors. We could tell a prospective donor that we served girls in every zip code in the country. We could talk about how many girls age 5 through 17 were involved, how many volunteers, and what kind of opportunities the girls had. But if anyone were to go around the United States asking Girl Scout people what we were doing and why it was beneficial to girls, a different answer might have come from each person. Not only was the public still carrying an image of Girl Scouts as little more than cookie salesgirls, but we couldn't even clarify our brand to ourselves.

Other Competition for Girls' Time and Attention

Every advance in communications technology in the past hundred years has opened doors for girls' activities. But cell phones and the Internet have blown those doors off the hinges. As a culture, America is swamped with information, images, expectations, and demands that our parents and grandparents couldn't have imagined. Girls are caught up and swept along "at the speed of girl." Their young minds are hard at work to learn this new stuff and take advantage of it for fun and a sense of belonging. The image of girls in a Girl Scout troop learning to tie knots or go camping seems dowdy to

girls who have many flashier and wider-reaching options for
how to spend their free time.

Girls need a reason to choose to get involved in any
organized activity. If they're not getting benefits that they
value, they'll just walk away. In 2004, girls' reasons to join
Girl Scouts weren't the same as a generation ago. And our
traditional offerings weren't keeping up with their new needs.

All Together Now

Girl Scouting was confronting brutal truths about problems
with how we conduct our business, interact with communities
and families, and attract and serve girls. Our GSRI research, and
our new strategy task force reaching out for input from Girl
Scout councils and from folks in other nonprofit youth services,
found pressing evidence that major change was essential to our
organization. We needed to reevaluate who our customer is,
and how to offer her a long-haul Girl Scout experience that's
relevant, meaningful, and cool. All the signs were telling us that
if we didn't do this, then business as usual would lead to no business at all. Girl Scouts' survival was at stake.

We had two options. One was to tackle our transformation
challenges one at a time. This seemed safe and doable, but it
would be slow and it would let critical problems fester. The
other option was to tackle all of our challenges at once: risky,
and maybe impossible.

We were lucky to be able to work directly with Willie
Pietersen (he is a faculty member at the Columbia University
School of Business in New York City) on Girl Scouts' reinven-
tion. The challenge of the Girl Scout transformation excited

Willie personally, both because we focus on developing leadership skills with people at a very young age and because of the vast under-representation of women in leadership positions in the workplace and in government.

One day, as Willie and I were shaping a list of recommendations, he said, "Do you realize you are sitting on one of the greatest moments of transformation? Are you ready for this? Do you have the stamina to take on this kind of massive change? It's going to take deep personal conviction, and monumental personal and organizational energy to pull this off." Willie was gearing up to help Girl Scouts do all the steps of transformation simultaneously. If we tackled issues piecemeal, it would never happen: one step would obscure the next, and by the time we got around to the final steps, the first would be obsolete again. Our end result would be just a shadow of what we intended and what we knew must be done. Incremental change couldn't possibly bring about the reinvention that would make Girl Scouting the world's best organization for girls. And no lesser goal made sense to us.

It was time to turn our girl-serving organization inside out. It was time to take a leap of faith, and be willing to follow through. We looked over the cliff and saw all those brutal truths below.

And we jumped.

6 "Trust Me, This Is Going to Work"

When Willie Pietersen started working with us, and I began to assemble 26 strategists from all over the country to envision Girl Scouts' future and shape a new core business strategy, Willie said, "That's way too many people." He thought it might be better to start with a small core team of senior executives, and get buy-in at that level before engaging a larger group in the process. I totally disagreed; I was convinced that we should jump in immediately with the larger team.

I explained that at the Girl Scouts, where volunteers outnumber paid staff a hundred to one, people at every level not only have an opinion, they expect it to be listened to. Our top brass can't just go off on their own and agree on a new process. "We are a highly inclusive, participatory organization," I told Willie. "Trust me, this is going to work."

Our 26-member strategy team came to New York for several three-day workshops in the initial planning phase. When we weren't meeting face-to-face, we were on conference calls. The group was thrilled to pioneer the future of Girl Scouting. Each member took that role seriously. Willie, whatever his private doubts, was intrigued to work with an iconic non-profit agency, so he restructured his process a bit to fit our ways of work. He became our guru-provocateur, challenging us to do our best thinking.

Initially he challenged us to come up with a reason for our existence: to define clearly what Girl Scouting is best in the world at (Jim Collins's hedgehog principle). We put the question to our councils. They sent in responses that varied a lot, but one theme ran through all of them: leadership. This resonated with our strategy team. Soon we had an answer to Willie's question. *What do we do? We develop leadership in girls.*

Who's the Customer?

Another challenge that Willie Pietersen posed for our strategy team was to identify our primary customer. I thought it would take two minutes to say "girls" and move on, but the team spent a lot of time going back and forth between girls and volunteers. Their indecision was a reminder of the challenges we were facing as an organization: if you don't know who you're trying to serve, how can you be effective at serving them?

There was logic behind the idea that our primary customer was the volunteers. One of Girl Scouting's historic guiding principles has always been: "The strength of the movement rests with the volunteers." Without volunteers, we'd have no program. We've always spent a lot of time providing help and guidance to volunteers, equipping them to make an impact in the lives of girls. We need to keep our one million volunteers happy, motivated, informed, and supplied with the tools of our trade.

But to what end? Our purpose for engaging volunteers is to bring girls into our program and give those girls a life-changing, life-building experience in the sisterhood of scouting. As the strategy group kept peeling back the layers of our reasoning, we finally came to agreement: the main purpose of Girl Scouts is to impact the girls. Volunteers are essential, but our true customers are the girls.

Was this discussion a waste of time? Did it prove Willie Pietersen right, that there were too many cooks in our kitchen? Not at all. It was a revealing moment for us; we realized that our movement gradually had become more volunteer-centered than girl-centered. But this wasn't going to get us where we needed to go, and it created a lot of unnecessary bureaucracy and cultural confusion. Now, as we came to realize that we had to be girl-focused, we gained a new way to see ourselves. If we introduce something new, our first question has to be: "What will girls think about this?" Because if our volunteers make choices that are best for themselves but in the long run turn girls off, they are doing something that runs counter to our very mission.

The Mission Statement

The early days of Girl Scouting, under the vision of Juliette Gordon Low, were times of adventure, breaking boundaries, and instilling confidence in girls so they could be change agents in their world. Juliette nurtured these values in girls before women had the right to vote. The first Girl Scout handbook (1913), *How Girls Can Help Their Country*, talks about being "handy" and strong, as well as about patriotism, camping, caring for the injured, the study of nature, and telling time by the stars. This handbook explored careers for girls, mentioning illustrious women who had taken up medicine, aviation, chemistry, and other fields.

"One individual," Juliette wrote, "often does more than a whole government or an army. One of you girls may some day alter the lives of hundreds of thousands of people. You know how one man invented printing; one woman started nursing the wounded as a profession for women; one man discovered America; one man invented steam engines; Galileo invented the telescope; Luther changed the life of Europe. So when you get an idea that will do good, follow it up, and don't fear that because it's only you that it cannot succeed."

Being a Girl Scout in Juliette Low's time meant being a pioneer. And it meant being brave; when Juliette said to fearlessly follow up on your good ideas, she meant it. The early Girl Scout troops weren't just about fun and social activities; they were about purpose, self-esteem, and a sense of belonging. Those Girl Scouts expected a lot from themselves and each other, at a time when most people didn't expect much from girls. Juliette Low took a revolutionary view of girls, and encouraged thousands of them to live out new possibilities. She shook up her era's status quo for girls.

The more I studied Juliette's message and the history of Girl Scouts, the more I saw that the Girl Scout movement had drifted, over the decades, from adventure to complacency, and from shaking up the status quo to riding along with it. This was partly because the country was coming to accept the idea of girls taking an active role in life, so Girl Scout activities like rock climbing, white-water rafting, and civic and volunteer service to communities didn't seem revolutionary anymore.

Yet girls and women still lacked anything like parity with boys and men. We'd come a long way, but we still weren't where we needed to be. Girl Scouting needed to reinvigorate Juliette's original vision as our driving force. We need to move our girls back out onto the cutting edge of essential risk taking. We need to make Girl Scouting revolutionary again.

Our 26-person strategy team, seeking input from all over and beyond the Girl Scout movement, discovered that most folks felt the time was ripe to transform the movement. And a powerful symbol of that resolve would be to revise the Girl Scout mission statement to more clearly tell the world our reason for being.

Girl Scouting had changed its mission statement several times before, to reflect the changing culture girls were growing up in. Here are some examples.

1912. To train girls to take their rightful places in life, first as good women, then as good citizens, wives, and mothers.

1924. The purpose of this organization is to help girls to realize the ideals of womanhood as a preparation for their responsibilities in the home and service to the community.

1957. We in Girl Scouting dedicate ourselves to the purpose of inspiring girls with the highest ideals of character, conduct, patriotism, and service that they may become happy and resourceful citizens.

Of course we still wanted girls to become happy and resourceful citizens, but we felt, in the spirit of Juliette, that we needed something with more zing to it. We asked for input from every level of Girl Scouting, and collected suggestions from hundreds of volunteers, staff members, and girls. Passions ran high about how, or even whether, to change the mission statement. Feedback suggested that it should say what girls get from their Girl Scout experience (personal development) and what they give back (community service), and that it should provide a simple definition of what we meant by leadership in Girl Scouting.

Mike and I and national board member Linda Foreman sat down to study all of the input, hoping to find a way to condense it to a simple sentence that you could easily see from across a room on a T-shirt. We boiled down the many pages of ideas to about 50 sentences or phrases. In the next pass we pruned everything down to a couple of dozen phrases, then printed them on a sheet of paper, cut each phrase out, and put the pieces on the floor to shuffle and try out different combinations.

It still was way too much to fit into a coherent sentence.

We performed triage, prioritizing which ideas were "must keep" and which were "also good." We reduced sentences to phrases, and phrases to single words, and at last we got a rough sentence:

Girl Scouting builds girls who are confident, who are courageous, who have character, and who make the world a better place.

It doesn't yet sing, does it? How about "Girl Scouting builds confident, courageous, character-filled girls who make the world a better place"? Not quite: we wanted "girls" to be in front, not hidden in the middle. And then we saw it: "Girl Scouting builds girls of C, C, and C. . . ."

What order should the three Cs go in? Confidence and character and courage were all equally important. We decided to put "courage" first, because the vowel-rhyme of "girls of courage" is memorable as you speak it. Then the rest came together:

Girl Scouting builds girls of courage, confidence, and character who make the world a better place.

This new mission statement emerged from thoughtful, passionate input of many, many caring Girl Scout volunteers and staff. The proof of their wisdom is that this mission statement has been happily accepted throughout Girl Scouting. Nearly everyone in our movement can quote it from memory—something that has never happened before in Girl Scouts' history.

Designing Our Strategy

Our strategy work looked at the big picture at first. We agreed on our essential purpose for being: to develop leadership in girls, and to become best in the world at doing that. Willie Pietersen helped us accept our brutal truths, which revealed five fundamental challenges in our organization. Through the summer and autumn of 2004 our strategy team, paying intense attention to feedback from all over the movement, crafted a new core business strategy to address those five challenges. At the end of the year, the team recommended five strategic priorities to GSUSA's national board:

Brand

We already had a nationally famous brand: the image of cute girls selling cookies and camping. That brand is ranked number 17 on the Cone Nonprofit Power Brand 100 list. Most organizations dream of having such a high-visibility brand. Yet that brand isn't consistent with our new decision about what Girl Scouting does best in the world; it isn't about leadership for girls. For our movement to make the leap from good to great, we need the public to see our renewed purpose. We need a compelling, contemporary brand that moves us from the "nice but not necessary" category for girls to the "I don't want to miss a minute" category. We must establish ourselves as important to girl culture across the country—and that doesn't mean just to girls. It means inspiring families to encourage their daughters to join, and volunteers to contribute time and energy, and donors to see leadership in girls as a critical need.

Program Model and Pathways

We need to build the world's best personal leadership development model for girls age 5 to 17. From that model, we need to produce a national program of learning activities, with clearly defined outcomes, differentiated by age level. We also must offer girls flexible pathways aside from our traditional troops, so they can take part in ways that make sense in their busy daily schedules. We need our programming to be more current, including dragging our Internet offerings kicking and screaming into the present day.

Governance and Organizational Structure

Girl Scouting's governance always has been democratic, and we won't compromise that. Yet we need our governance to be efficient and effective as well, and that means becoming flexible and nimble in making decisions for policy and business. Furthermore, the leadership that we show at the top of the organization needs to positively reflect the leadership model we aim to instill in girls.

Oh, and, um, er, we might want to take (shhh!) a little look at how our 312-council structure is, or isn't, doing the best possible job (watch out for elephants!) of delivering scouting to girls.

Volunteerism

We need to attract, retain, and motivate a cadre of diverse volunteers who mirror the demography of the nation's girls. We need to make it easier for volunteers to lead troops. And just as we need to develop new ways and new motives for girls to join and take part, we also need to make it possible and attractive for adults who don't have time to become troop leaders to exercise their support for girls by taking part in other ways in the Girl Scout movement.

Funding

Our traditional economic model simply can't fund the wide range of things we know we must do for girls. In order to deliver programs that twenty-first-century girls need, and to reach the number of girls who need them (hey, why not aim for two or three times as many girls as we're reaching now?), we're going to have to communicate with donors, including our 50 million Girl Scout alumnae, and convince them that investing in girls is essential to our country's future.

Closing the Gap

It's one thing to say, "Here's where we are now, and here's where we need to leap to," and quite another to figure out how to get across the gap.

Once the strategy team recommended its five priorities to the board, we closed down that team and formed five new "gap teams." Each was assigned to focus on one of the five priorities of the core business strategy and figure out how we were going to close the gap between our current condition and the one we aspired to.

At this point the transformation was turning scary-real to us. Instead of talking about the big picture, which is exciting and doesn't cost anything, we would now be talking about the smaller picture, which could directly affect people's jobs and lives. Our gap-leaping process had to fairly meet the needs of small and large Girl Scout councils, urban and rural areas, ethnic diversity, and constraints of geography. Everyone in the movement had to feel that her voice was heard in this process. So the gap teams had to be large: eventually 76 people took part in them.

The gap teams started their work in February 2005. In July, they came together to report their recommendations.

The program group said we needed an entirely new program model for girls: new handbooks, materials, and activities; outcomes-based learning progression by age level; new structures for program delivery to girls; and new training for volunteers and staff nationwide.

The brand and funding teams didn't report at this meeting—it was too early for them, since we didn't yet have the infrastructure in place to really do their work. The volunteer-ism team reported, but briefly; a lot of what they needed to do would have to wait until the new program was in place.

Then the elephant in the room put its foot down.

The Elephant in the Room

The structure and governance gap team, like the other four, comprised representatives from Girl Scout councils of all shapes and sizes from both coasts and everywhere between. This gap team told us that we needed to downsize our national structure of Girl Scout councils into fewer, larger councils that could provide better services to girls.

Downsize? The gap team wasn't talking about trimming fat. They recommended that we massively reduce the number of councils.

I already knew what they were going to say, because I'd been tipped off. And a lot of other people had already been thinking along these lines and conversing about it under the radar. Shortly before I arrived as CEO, the national board had quietly engaged the consulting firm Grant Thornton to look into what the right council structure might be. But until this moment, nobody had said it out loud. The idea was so obvious, and at the same time so huge and complicated and potentially disruptive, that no one wanted to be the first to bring it out into the open.

However, we knew that Girl Scouting had survived downsizing once before. In the early days, Girl Scouting had grown so fast and spread so far that there had been no time to stop and define exactly what a Girl Scout council should be. Five years after Juliette Low formed her first troop of 18 girls in Savannah, there already was a Girl Scout council in Hawaii. By 1940, 1,700 independent corporations in the United States were calling themselves Girl Scout councils.

Between 1940 and 1960, in a long, slow, painful consolidation process known as Green Umbrella, GSUSA combined those 1,700 councils into 400 councils. Periodic mergers over the next four decades brought the number down to 312 by the time I became national CEO.

Still, too many councils had such a small budget or staff that they couldn't give girls the best possible Girl Scout experience. Fewer, stronger councils that combined the resources and territories of the weaker ones could do a better job. Many of us knew this. Yet no one had publicly raised the issue until the gap team elephant stamped its foot.

Audible gasps echoed in the room, and then deafening silence. A moment of truth had arrived: either we were going to achieve true transformation or we weren't.

Damage Control

It was almost paralyzing to think how much was at stake if we did as the gap team said. Staff at councils all over the country would see their jobs or their office locations change. Agonizing decisions must be made about who must merge with whom. Council traditions would be cast aside, and identities lost. And for the first time in scouting history, we'd have to buckle down and describe what a "high-capacity" Girl Scout council should look like and what its infrastructure should be.

Our immediate problem was how to publicly announce the gap team's recommendation. The national board president and I huddled to make a plan before anyone left the conference center. If we let the news just leak out about massive reorganization, the story would take on a life of its own—or rather a hundred lives of their own, all different and all upsetting. So we created an e-mail with PowerPoint, and sent it out quickly so each council could share it with its staff and volunteers. This presentation told what had been suggested, and made it clear that the idea was under discussion and no official decision had been made.

Response from council staff, boards, and volunteers was all over the place. Some councils said it was about time we seriously looked at this. Others resisted the idea and asked for hard-and-fast proof that a new plan would be an improvement over what was already in place. There was also concern that the whole thing would be mandated by Girl Scouts of the USA without allowing councils to have a say.

Overall, though, the feedback wasn't waving a huge red flag to stop the conversation. Folks were coming to terms with the idea that restructure had to be considered.

A nationwide conversation about merging into fewer and bigger high-capacity councils began as we headed for the October 2005 National Council Session, a triennial meeting where delegates from all the councils gather to vote on Girl Scout policy changes. A month before that meeting, GSUSA hired professional demographers to recommend how to draw the boundary lines of the proposed new Girl Scout councils. We let all councils know that, in addition to asking Girl Scout staff and volunteers to send us their own opinions, we also were seeking this objective analysis.

At the National Council Session, 1,800 Girl Scout delegates voted to approve the new focus of Girl Scouting, including the new mission statement.

For the next two months, the gap teams refined their "how to get there" tactics. Now everyone was looking forward to another big national meeting in the spring, where the proposed map of new high-capacity councils—with specific council boundaries being set, all across the country—would be unveiled.

Redrawing the Map

In the months between the gap team report and the National Council Session, we asked councils, "If our national council structure is redesigned, what should a redesigned council look like?" We gave a list of structural qualities, for respondents to rank in order of priority. The councils' response, along with input from the demographers, helped us create a profile of a high-capacity council based on available resources, funding base, state lines, school district boundaries, population diversity (current and projected), transportation patterns, natural geographic boundaries, and major media markets. To this we added size requirements: each new council must serve an area where at least 100,000 girls age 5 through 17 live and there's at least $15 billion in total household income and at least one city of 50,000 or more residents.

In March 2006, we held a specially called meeting of the CEOs and board chairs of all 312 Girl Scout councils. The two demographers we'd hired—who looked poignantly small and human as they stood onstage beside a covered easel and addressed more than 600 nervous Girl Scout council leaders—told of the reasoning that had gone into their map of new councils. As they spoke, a murmur swept through the room. You could see heads nodding as people quietly agreed that the demographers were talking sense, and their description of a high-capacity Girl Scout council sounded like the right way to serve girls.

Still, no one knew what the new map would look like, or how 200 corporate mergers could be accomplished; how council staffs and boards could be reorganized, and scores of jobs could be shifted or lost; how hundreds of camp and office properties could be transferred; how a century of traditional identities could be resurrected in the new format.

The demographers took a deep breath and flipped the cover backward off the map, which suddenly appeared on jumbotrons flanking the stage. It showed that 29 current councils already met the capacity criteria and did not need to be merged. The remaining 283 would be realigned into 80 larger councils, for a new total of 109 councils across the country.

There was breathtaking silence as every council CEO and board chair took a first instant to see what it meant not just for the organization, but for them personally. Slowly someone started to clap. Then the room erupted in a standing ovation. My heart nearly burst with admiration for these remarkable women who were applauding themselves and each other for having the courage to tackle such a huge issue. There was a sense in the room—and in feedback afterward from all parties—that everyone needed to get on board because it was the right thing to do for our millions of girls. Eighteen council leaders came forward immediately and said, "This makes so much sense, let us be early adopters to go through the process first. We'll help you figure it out for the rest of them."

During the next two months, we gave the councils time to make their own recommendations if they disagreed with the demographers' map. A few suggestions made sense— people who live in a place may understand things in ways demographers can't—so we adjusted a handful of boundary lines. But when the national board approved the new map in

August 2006, it looked very similar to the one on the easel. And councils felt that their input had been fairly considered.

After that, the process went quickly. Within two years, more than half the mergers were done. By 2009 all Girl Scouts in the United States were served by 112 councils. From the first stirrings of "The status quo has got to go" in 2004, it took just five years for our unwieldy, tradition-bound organization to conceive, propose, discuss, plan, and actually do the whole merger process.

Not all the kinks are worked out yet. One small council is legally fighting its merger as this book goes to press, and the challenge of getting all the new councils operating at peak performance is ongoing. But the speed and goodwill with which Girl Scouting reorganized its council structure is a testimony to the grit and heart of all Girl Scout leaders, and to their willingness to put the good of girls above their own preferences.

It's also a tribute to their leadership ability. Any time you hear anyone disparage women as leaders or say that women dither and won't make hard decisions, tell them to come talk to Girl Scouts. Those council leaders were some tough cookies.

The Human Factor

GSUSA wasn't prepared, in-house, to implement the restructuring, so we hired consultants who were known and respected for their understanding of mergers. These consultants trained a pool of Girl Scout staff who helped with the process. We designed and distributed workbooks to all councils, showing them step-by-step how to merge in a collaborative way that would produce the best outcomes for girls.

The question of who would be CEO of each new council was handled this way. First a leadership team was created for each jurisdictional change. A CEO search process was designed. In cases where multiple CEOs wanted to stay in leadership in one of the merged councils, we designed a consistent process for the final decision. We couldn't make it painless, but we tried to make it fair.

Once again I credit how immensely helpful were the courageous and mission-focused CEOs who willingly put the greater good above their personal interests. Many had been career Girl Scout professionals for 15 or 20 years, and most of them were personal friends of mine. We couldn't keep them all in place; but in some cases, new jobs were created in the merged councils, and the former CEOs found places there. Some didn't, and this part of it was hard for me and very painful for the ones who had to leave the movement. Yet they handled it with great dignity, and Girl Scouting owes them all a debt. (On the bright side, other companies who have hired those women are now benefiting from their character and ability.)

As you open this book, Girl Scouting is beginning to see the growth and maturity of our new council structure. Most people who work with mergers say it takes at least three to five years before you start to see the real benefits, and our own mergers took place as the country was tumbling into the worst economic slump in generations. I shudder to think what challenges we would face now if we had delayed a year or two to begin, or if our stalwart council staffs and boards hadn't completed the mergers so promptly.

On Beyond Planning

One thing that has been fundamentally different and constantly unsettling as we've worked toward our new core business strategy is that for 90 years the goal-setting process in Girl Scouting has focused on a 12-month calendar. Our membership will increase by *this* much by *this* certain date. We will raise *this* much funding. But going into the transformation process, when we realized that incrementalism couldn't get us where we needed to go, the time frame flipped. Instead of imposing our timing on events, events imposed their timing on us.

We went into our transformation not knowing how long each of the strategic priorities would take to accomplish. We just knew that each of them needed to be done, and that doing them all at once was the only way to achieve them all. Eight years later, still in the process, we are further along on some priorities than on others, but solidly committed to continue until all are fully realized.

The transformation of Girl Scouting has been tremendously exciting. I can't say that I came into the job ready to try to do it. At the 2003 Council CEO Summit—while I was still CEO of the Girl Scout council in middle Tennessee— management experts from Stanford University led all the council leaders in a discussion of Girl Scouting's core purpose. The Stanford people challenged us to answer the question: "What are you in business to do?" We council CEOs were not able to provide a cohesive answer. We couldn't come up with any sort of consensus at all. We were all motivated and committed to serve girls, but we still couldn't organize our decisions around our purpose.

A year later, as the new national CEO, when I sensed a willingness in the movement to make radical change, I understood that we were holding in our hands the legacy of Juliette Gordon Low, along with the hopes and dreams of more than 90 years of dedicated women who had followed her vision. It was time for us to do whatever it would take to get us, and the millions of girls we serve, to and through the organization's next hundred years.

7 What to Keep, and What to Let Go

The Girl Scout Promise

On my honor, I will try:
To serve God and my country,
To help people at all times,
And to live by the Girl Scout Law.

The Girl Scout Law

I will do my best to be
honest and fair,
friendly and helpful,
considerate and caring,
courageous and strong, and
responsible for what I say and do,
and to
respect myself and others,
respect authority,
use resources wisely,
make the world a better place, and
be a sister to every Girl Scout.

Girl Scouting's transformation started as we were approaching our 100th birthday. The anniversary, in 2012, would be a great opportunity to tell the world about the new Girl Scouting. For many of us, it would mark the real beginning of our new era. As we approached this milestone, we began looking with new eyes at our traditions, to decide what to take with us into the next century and what to leave behind.

One thing we will surely take with us is the spirit of our founder, Juliette Gordon Low. Juliette didn't invent scouting—it was already a growing movement when she got to England—but she seized the torch and carried it far beyond where she found it. And she did it in a hurry, in a life that ended too soon. Fifteen years after founding Girl Scouts of the USA, Juliette died of breast cancer.

During those 15 years she was fearless. When she committed to establish Girl Scouting, she plunged in heedless of obstacles. In Juliette's time, girls weren't supposed to be active, much less camp out in wilderness. The races weren't supposed to mix as equals, nor were people of different social classes. Physically handicapped people were supposed to stay out of sight and not disturb the healthy. Juliette's challenge to all these assumptions put her in the revolutionary company of American activist women like Harriet Beecher Stowe, Carrie Nation, Sojourner Truth, Clara Barton, Susan B. Anthony, and Ida Tarbell. Juliette's "defy convention" spirit always will be essential in our movement.

Another facet of Girl Scouting we'll keep is the central involvement of volunteers. Juliette knew from the start that scouting depended on volunteers to give their time and attention to help girls, and she focused her energy on serving the needs of girls *and* volunteers. It's a tricky balancing act; the girls have to come first, but when girls learn about courage, confidence, character, and making the world a better place, they learn it from their hands-on role models. So the movement must build those qualities in its volunteers as well, helping each to find the leader within herself through encouragement and training and opportunities to stretch and grow. Juliette herself was a great role model for Girl Scout volunteers: in her first 50 years, she lived a privileged life of little purpose; in her last 15, she volunteered to create the world's largest and most effective organization for girls.

As I know from my own mother, and from thousands of Girl Scout volunteers it has been my privilege to meet, becoming a Girl Scout troop leader is a life changer for women. You get an opportunity to build your organizational skills, become a better public speaker, learn conflict resolution, and get better at setting short-term and long-term goals—all while making a difference in the lives of a group of growing girls. While running the Girl Scout council in Nashville, I met many troop leaders who decided to go back to college after they got involved with running a Girl Scout troop, or they got an important job promotion, or they led a big charity fund-raiser.

As we looked to our 100th birthday, we knew that revolutionary vision and a bedrock commitment to girls and to volunteers are two things we definitely are bringing with us into Girl Scouts' new century.

The Magic Circle

Courage and commitment shine in Girl Scout activities and especially in our ceremonies and rituals that tie today's girls to each other and to the Girl Scouts of the past. When I think back on my days as a young Girl Scout—this is a story that every former Girl Scout will tell you—the rites and ceremonies are some of the things I remember most vividly and that meant the most to me at the time. Those ritualized moments of sisterhood gave me a sense of belonging, of being part of something larger than myself. In 2004 as we envisioned Girl Scouting's future, we knew that these life-changing ceremonies are, and always will be, fundamental to Girl Scouting.

One important ritual is reciting the Promise and Law at each troop meeting. I recall a swell of pride that I felt, as a girl, to recommit to the Girl Scout Law each time. It was something that made Girl Scouting more than just an after-school activity for me.

Girls' connection to the Promise and Law never goes away. We have a saying, "Once a Girl Scout, always a Girl Scout"; I saw proof of that when Frances Hesselbein gave the keynote address at the historic meeting where the demographers unveiled the new map of Girl Scout councils. Frances ended her speech by lowering her voice to a whisper and saying, slowly and clearly, "On my honor, I will try. . . ."

There wasn't a dry eye in the house; it moved us when we were girls, and it moves us now. It connects us with every girl who, at age 5 or 6, learns to recite that Promise with her sister Girl Scouts. And "On my honor" still reminds us to strive for the best in everything we do.

There are Girl Scout rituals that are turning points in girls' lives, like bridging ceremonies, when a girl graduates to the next level in the scouting experience. I remember taking off my Brownie beanie and crossing that little bridge to the other side, where my Girl Scout sash was waiting for me. It meant I was growing up.

In 2007 the Girl Scout council in San Francisco hosted a huge bridging ceremony on the Golden Gate Bridge. Many thousands of girls came from all over the region and held hands, spanning the entire length of the bridge. The news photos were amazing. The girls' faces, glowing in a brisk breeze, showed their joy at this once-in-a-lifetime affirmation of their place in a sisterhood that stretched farther than their eyes could see.

At our Girl Scout conference venue, the Edith Macy Center in rural New York State, there is a venerable stone-and-wood Great Hall from which Juliette Gordon Low used to lead candle-carrying girls through a doorway, along a

winding path, and down steps, each of which signified steps
in the Girl Scout journey. Whenever I walk that path and
imagine those girls—some of whom are still living today at an
age as old as Juliette's dream—I am moved to tears of grati-
tude for what I am privileged to be part of.

For many girls, the stepping-up ceremonies of Girl Scouts
mark otherwise hard-to-come-by guideposts on the path to
becoming an adult. Some cultures have moving occasions like
the bat mitzvah, confirmation, or *quinceañera* to mark such
passages. For many girls across the United States, though,
Girl Scouts is a rare place to feel that passage and that growth.
Scouting's rituals help girls reflect on past achievements and
look ahead to new challenges, experiences, and levels of
responsibility.

Adults experience Girl Scout rituals at our corporate level,
too. We do investiture ceremonies for new employees. We get
in a circle and light a candle for each part of the Girl Scout
Law, and pin them and do the Girl Scout handshake. It's a
simple thing, but I've yet to see a new employee not be moved
by it. The moment says to them, "You belong to something
bigger than you are."

Speaking of belonging, another thing we're taking with
us into the next century is Juliette's focus on diversity. A key
value of Girl Scouting is to be open to all girls and to embrace
the variety of our country's people. We welcome any girl who
will keep the Promise, live by the Law, and be a sister to every
other Girl Scout. This is a great strength of our organization.
It's good for all our girls to be with girls who are different
from themselves in background and interests and life experiences. The more we learn how to get along with people from

all walks of life and appreciate their unique abilities and life views, the better off we all are.

Our appreciation of diversity plays out in the symbolism of the circle, which will continue as part of Girl Scout activities and ceremonies. The friendship circle, often done at the end of a meeting, represents an unbroken chain of camaraderie: the circle has no end. It's also a visual reminder that all the girls are on level ground. Nobody is in front, and nobody is behind.

In my former Nashville office there's an engraved saying over the receptionist's desk: "Our world is a circle of friendship united by ideals." Every morning when I went to work there, that phrase welcomed me into Girl Scouting's sisterhood.

Dressing the Part

Girl Scout uniforms have long been a powerful unifying symbol for our girls and volunteers. As we began planning the transformation in Girl Scouting, we opened a national conversation about whether and how to continue the tradition of uniforms. We got passionate feedback. Some people felt the idea of wearing uniforms was outdated, or that girls might no longer feel a uniform cool to wear. Others, especially longtime Girl Scout volunteers, would rather lose their skin than their uniform. And some pointed out that the uniform is a symbol of equality: no girl is dressed better or worse than any of her sister Girl Scouts.

Girl Scout uniforms have changed over the years. On our walls at GSUSA headquarters are photographs of the

National Council Sessions of bygone years, where thousands
of Girl Scout delegates and volunteers from councils all over
the country gathered to exercise democracy in planning the
future of the movement. In the earliest photos, you'll see
ankle-length khaki skirts, campaign hats (like army drill ser-
geants) and high-button collars, reflecting the military origin
of Boy and Girl Scouts' mode of dress. In those photos, you
can't miss the pride and birds-of-a-feather importance of the
uniform.

Over the years we have adjusted the hem, the hue, and
the style. But looking to our second century, we needed to
seriously consider how uniforms might or might not fit into a
new era in which girls are finding many other ways to express
their identity and their interpersonal connections.

To assess how to dress Girl Scouts in the future, we
looked to our past. In the 1920s, military khakis gave way to
pleated bloomers (only for camping). When Brownies (second
and third grades) became part of scouting, the new age level
got its trademark brown uniform complete with a generous
hem to accommodate a growing child, and that famous little
beanie cap. Later, green cotton replaced khaki for older girls,
and we introduced "action pleats," zippers, insignia sashes and
vests, mix-and-match pieces, and skirts that could be worn
over shorts and easily removed for hiking and sports.

In 2004 as we began Girl Scouting's transformation,
many were willing to change the uniforms. Some were willing to dispense with them or make them optional. The
opinions that poured in from all over Girl Scouting were so
conflicting that GSUSA could not decide what to do.

Finally we stopped asking each other, and asked the girls instead.

Girls answered in two ways. On one hand, uniforms were a barrier to many of the older girls. They wanted to be involved with the program and they liked what Girl Scouts was about, but they were embarrassed to have to wear a uniform in front of outsiders and run a risk of being thought dorky or uncool. Younger girls, on the other hand, loved the idea of uniforms and definitely wanted to wear them.

We came down firmly on both sides of the question. Uniforms are now required only for the youngest girls, the Daisy Girl Scouts (kindergarten and first grade) and Brownie Girl Scouts. Even there we allow latitude. There are Daisy pinafores, for example, and Brownie skirts and shorts, and beanies. Each older age level (Juniors, grades 4 and 5; Cadettes, grades 6 through 8; Seniors, grades 9 and 10; and the new Ambassadors, grades 11 and 12) has at least one required element—a sash or a vest—upon which the girls display badges and awards. Beyond that, Juniors, Cadettes, Seniors, and Ambassadors now buy their own white shirts and khaki slacks or skirts. When the girls gather "in uniform" they wear a vest or a sash with their badges on it. To be out of uniform, they need only pop the vest or sash into their backpacks and become, to an outside observer, a kid dressed like all the other kids.

At big Girl Scout events, it's still a beautiful sight to see hundreds of teen girls proudly sporting vests and sashes loaded with badges and pins.

Adult volunteers, when they're on official Girl Scout business, wear a navy suit with a specially designed Girl Scout scarf. For other Girl Scout occasions, a wide array of official T-shirts and other casual clothing is available for volunteers.

In our new century, girls and women of all ages dress in ways that make them feel comfortable and proud to be Girl Scouts.

Gathering the Troops

A powerful Girl Scout tradition is the long-lasting bond between the girls and their troop leaders. In our traditional program delivery model, a volunteer who gains a certain

amount of experience working on Girl Scout events or assist-
ing in troop activities becomes a troop leader. Guided by
council staff or senior volunteers, she is assigned a group
of girls in, say, second and third grade (Brownie Girl Scout
age level) who become her troop. The troop meets weekly
or every couple of weeks throughout the school year, with
the girls doing activities and learning skills to qualify to earn
badges and awards. Troops sometimes stay together for years,
with the leaders learning to teach new skills as the girls grow.
Troops have always been the way Girl Scouting is delivered to
most of our girl members.

But the troop model puts a burden of time and energy
commitment on the troop leader, and troop meetings depend
on girls having schedules that allow an hour or two a week,
plus time for outside activities at camp and on the cookie sale
and in community action projects.

In the early and middle decades of the twentieth century,
the troop model was the usual way for girls and families to
engage in scouting. But as families began to need two wage
earners, and as kids' time was diverted by a growing variety
of activities, fewer adults and kids had as much free time, and
our number of girls in troops began to decline. Also, girls in
middle school and high school seemed to be psychologically
outgrowing the troop model. We realized that we need other
ways for girls and volunteers to experience Girl Scouting; and
girls and adults were telling us that they wanted to take part if
we could offer different ways to do it. Another problem with
troops was that the public generally saw them as white and
suburban, an image unlikely to attract girls from low-income
and rural areas and families of various ethnicities. As an

organization that values diversity, we needed to find ways to attract and serve all girls.

Outreach

I was a council CEO during the 1980s and 1990s when *outreach* became a buzzword in our movement. Councils strove to revive their shrinking membership by involving diverse girls in short-term or one-time activities. These activities didn't last all year or provide ongoing development and sisterhood like troops did, but they increased our membership by, for example, getting a hundred new girls to attend a two-day theme camp on science or math.

Along with other council CEOs, I jumped on this bandwagon. We went out into our communities and brought girls in, and they came in droves. The community loved for us to do this kind of event. Everyone was dazzled by the contemporary and innovative offerings and the partnerships we were creating. There were sports days, math and science programs, business training opportunities—a wide variety of activities.

The events might last just a few hours or continue for up to six weeks. My council signed up 500 new Girl Scouts for an all-day-Saturday entrepreneurial event in Nashville, called *Income of Her Own,* where girls talked with area businesswomen about business planning, designing business cards, building résumés, and the challenges of succeeding as women in high-profile careers. The girls and the businesswomen loved it, and it felt great to make an impact in these girls' lives and give them a new wider perception of their own possibilities.

Sometimes, due to funding or government regulations, outreach events had to include boys as well. Involving boys didn't support Girl Scouting's all-girl environment, but we figured our brand was strong enough to withstand the occasional change.

The outreach events seemed like a great strategy at the time; we were creating rich encounters for girls and exposing them to interesting, challenging, relevant experiences. But there were problems. One was that girls were signing up for the individual events, but that event was the first and last time we ever saw them. Our membership rose on paper, but the new members were Girl Scouts for only days or hours.

And many of the programs weren't sustainable. A council might obtain special funding for events and get a bump in membership numbers, but the next year the funding wouldn't be available and the events wouldn't happen, and the council would show a sudden drop in membership.

Our intentions were good, and the outreach programs did give a lot of new girls exciting experiences and a touch of Girl Scouting. But the outreach approach to Girl Scouting was fragmenting our program. It was part of the status quo that we had to let go.

(Some short-term, individual outreach programs are still going on and are offering immediate benefits for girls. But as a long-term way to deliver consistent and measurable outcomes, they fall short of what we need.)

So if the troop model—which still works beautifully for many girls (especially younger girls) and will be a big part of Girl Scouting in the new century—has a hard time thriving in an environment in which girls and families are busier and more diverse, and if the outreach model isn't a lasting, progressive learning experience, then how can we best deliver our leadership program to girls?

As we asked ourselves that question, we decided that whatever delivery model we used, our program for girls needed to be a nationally consistent portfolio of activities and materials that felt, to every girl who took part, like Girl Scouting and not like just some random learning event.

We also decided that serving boys with Girl Scout programming really wasn't Girl Scouting. A fundamental thing Girl Scouting does for girls is give them a safe place to try, fail, and try again in a supportive all-girl environment without worrying what boys think or say. If a council wants to do an event that brings in boys and families to build relationships, that's fine, but otherwise we shouldn't run coed activities.

Pathways

As with our decision about uniforms, the question "How do we deliver Girl Scouting?" has more than one answer. We're developing what we call pathways by which girls can enjoy scouting. Each pathway incorporates our new program's *Discover, Connect, Take Action* keys to developing leadership in girls. Each pathway is girl-led, in an all-girl environment, where girls learn by doing, in activities that take place over time. Each pathway is accessible and relevant to all girls. Each pathway includes consistent volunteer training opportunities.

What do the pathways look like? Troops are a pathway. For girls and adults who have the time and commitment, troops still are a great way to deliver a long-term Girl Scout program and keep girls involved for years. Day camp and resident camp also are pathways. Other examples are specialized activity programs that we call the special interest leadership pathway, the travel leadership pathway, the virtual leadership pathway, and the service leadership pathway. Here's an example. Cynthia, in fifth grade, may transition from her troop to an outdoor pathway where she attends a spring break camp with girls from across her region, completes a counselor-in-training program, and volunteers as a camp counselor at a summer resident camp for Brownie Girl Scouts.

Short-term events that we still offer are different from one-time membership-boost outreach programs. We run recruitment events that are open to all girls, to introduce potential members to the Girl Scout experience and encourage them to register as Girl Scouts and take part in multiple events during the year. Our short-term Girl Scout events and activities are designed so girls who don't follow up afterward still get a much more consistent taste of scouting than they got in the past.

We no longer recruit girls without a plan for their ongoing involvement and membership.

Taking New Journeys

Our core business strategy has driven big changes in our program for girls. We realized we needed programs that could build on girls' past scouting experiences, resonate with diverse populations, incorporate service and citizenship and community action, and produce consistent experiences and outcomes. These guidelines led us to design and introduce leadership "journeys"—books of activities, lessons, and games—for girls of different ages. Each journey offers progressive activities related to a theme. For example, in the journey series *It's Your Planet—Love It!*, Brownie Girl Scouts learn about the importance of water, its scarcity, and how to conserve it, and they create their own service projects to educate friends and the community. One Brownie troop took the lessons they learned in their journey, and created and produced a public service announcement about how to conserve water; they got it featured on their local television stations, and they used it in schools to educate students.

Each journey is also tied to specific outcomes—such as "Girls can solve conflicts"—enabling us for the first time in scouting's history to say to families, donors, and legislators, "Here's what girls get out of Girl Scouting." Identifying and quantifying those outcomes has been a major challenge; I'll tell you more about it in the next chapter. We're still in the early stages of this work, but the evidence we've gathered so far is encouraging. Council leaders and volunteers are telling us they can see the program making girls stronger and more confident.

As I look at what we're taking with us as we go forward, I think back again to Juliette Low. As Girl Scouting enters its second century, we are blending cutting-edge practices with Juliette's revolutionary spirit, and with the best and truest elements of our past. Juliette might be a little cranky about the uniforms—she loved her Girl Scout uniform so much she asked to be buried in it—but overall I think she'd be proud of us.

8 Oh, Yeah? Prove It!

If we go to families and say, "Your girls should join Girl Scouts because . . ." or if we tell donors, "You should give to Girl Scouts because your gift will accomplish . . ." or if we lobby legislators to "Support a program that favors girls and women because it will . . ."—the end of our sentence had better be really convincing.

It's a tough challenge to measure the effect of a social service program. You have to chronicle a lot of people over a long period of time to discover the results. That's expensive to do, and it's hard work. It's much easier to do social research in a snapshot way: on a given day, you ask X people what they think of Y, and you publish the result.

Fortunately, we already have some long-term evidence of Girl Scouting's success. Though only 10 percent of American girls have been Girl Scouts at any one time, 80 percent of female senior executives and business owners are former Girl Scouts. Two-thirds of the women in Congress and virtually all of the women in NASA's astronaut corps are former Girl Scouts. Our alumnae cluster at the top of practically every profession.

In general ways, we know how we've achieved this. But in 2004 as we shifted our brand to "leadership for girls," we knew we'd need to show our constituents solid evidence that we do it better than any other organization they can steer their girls toward or give their funding to. Saying "Girl Scouting builds girls of courage, confidence, and character who make the world a better place" isn't enough. We have to prove it.

Suppose you set a goal to drive to Chicago. You gas up the car and head out. Along the way you see signs telling you you're getting closer. When you see the big lake and a lot of tall buildings and signs that say WELCOME TO CHICAGO, you have good evidence that you've succeeded.

Evidence may be trickier to find when your goal is organizational transformation. But even there, a lot of your progress is measurable. If you aim to merge 312 councils into 109, and five years later you have 112 councils, that's evidence of progress.

If your goal is to develop leadership in girls, it can be a real challenge to measure your progress. Our alumnae's achievements are evidence of our past success. But how do you look at a new leadership program *while you're delivering it to young girls* and see whether those girls are on the right track?

Starting to Measure Outcomes

To measure the benefits that girls get from their Girl Scout experience, we need to ask a lot of girls a lot of specific questions. We aren't trying to grade girls or volunteers on how they're doing—not now, not ever. We just need to judge how well our program does what it's designed to do: build girls of courage, confidence, and character who make the world a better place.

How do you measure courage in a nine-year-old girl? Leadership? Confidence? You can do it by measuring behaviors: what a certain girl does in a certain situation, and what's different about what she does this year from what she did last year. This analysis of behaviors isn't rocket science—every parent knows that some behaviors are good signs and some are bad signs—but it is, in fact, science. Studies in many fields prove that certain behaviors mean certain development has taken place.

So we have a place to start that isn't reliant on guesswork.

We've begun our measurements by asking an advisory board of experts in child development and education, "If you were designing a program to strengthen girls in three specific development areas, what would you actually do for them?" The three areas are the three elements of our *Discover, Connect, Take Action* leadership model: developing girls who know and trust themselves (discover self), who understand how to build healthy relationships (connect with others), and who are interested to work for the good of something larger than themselves (take action to serve their communities).

The experts' response has led us to create a list of 15 outcomes of such a program—five in each area—that the experts agree, "Yes, if a girl develops in these ways, she will in fact discover herself, connect with others, and take action to improve her community. Her leadership abilities will be highly developed." Here's the list:

Girls Discover Self

- Girls develop a strong sense of self.
- Girls develop positive values.

- Girls gain practical life skills.
- Girls seek challenges in the world.
- Girls develop critical thinking.

Girls Connect with Others

- Girls develop healthy relationships.
- Girls promote cooperation and team building.
- Girls can resolve conflicts.
- Girls advance diversity in a multicultural world.
- Girls feel connected to their communities, locally and globally.

Girls Take Action in Service

- Girls can identify community needs.
- Girls are resourceful problem solvers.
- Girls advocate for themselves and others, locally and globally.
- Girls educate and inspire others to act.
- Girls feel empowered to make a difference in the world.

Sounds good, doesn't it? It's an expanded version of our mission statement. But it's still not something you can measure. Does Cassandra have a strong sense of self? *Why, yes, she does; thank you for asking.* How do you know? *Well, um. . . .*

This is where the behaviors come in.

Our team came up with a list of goals for each age group, and a set of behavior indicators that can show whether these goals are being met. For example, let's suppose a goal is for

Anna, a Daisy Girl Scout in kindergarten, to develop a stronger sense of self. That means we want Anna to achieve the outcome of being better able to recognize her own strengths and abilities. A behavior that we can observe, to tell us that Anna is achieving that outcome, would be that she makes positive statements about her abilities or shows others what she can do.

If Anna behaves in those ways more at the end of a school year than she did at the beginning, she's making measurable progress. If she shows behavioral progress on most or all of a spectrum of related indicators, we have measurable evidence that our program is working for Anna.

If most or all of the girls in Anna's troop also are showing that kind of progress, it's an encouraging sign that our overall program is working. If all of the 10,000 girls in Anna's council, from Daisy to Ambassador, are making progress, it's a *very* encouraging sign. And if Anna's progress is repeated council by council throughout the movement, we have evidence to share with volunteers, parents, donors, and educators that the Girl Scout leadership program actually accomplishes great things for girls.

We're just beginning to gather the detailed, nationwide evidence that can prove our case. But already, volunteers who work with the new leadership journeys are telling us that they're really starting to see the program make a difference with the girls.

We'll keep refining our leadership program (with girls' help) and we'll keep measuring the outcomes. This is groundbreaking work in the nonprofit sector and it can help pave a way to encourage progress on many girls' and women's issues.

Vision, Constant Learning, and Optimism

Girls aren't the only ones who are taking our leadership journey. The transformation work we've been doing has changed our organization and our volunteers, by encouraging all of us toward continuous learning: trying, stumbling, trying again, learning, and then trying again and learning more.

And of course, the more you learn, the more you can dream.

Being a constant learner and being a visionary go hand in hand. For example, as a troop leader, your active learning helps you figure out how to take your troop in the direction that your vision (and your girls' vision) tells you it should go.

Your own active learning also helps you keep up with the girls. If you don't keep learning constantly, the girls will leave you in the dust.

I saw a powerful example of this through the eyes of a friend and her daughter. Andrea began leading a troop of Brownie Girl Scouts a few years ago that included her daughter Samantha. The girls became fascinated with the idea that girls in other countries shared their sisterhood of scouting. They studied about Girl Scouts' parent organization, the World Association of Girl Guides and Girl Scouts. They decided to do a troop activity celebrating World Thinking Day. Each girl brought food and a game representing a different country, and they invited a few friends. The next year, the girls did another World Thinking Day event, and it was bigger. By the time they entered middle school, their troop's World Thinking Day event had turned into a community-wide celebration with hundreds of people enjoying programs that the girls presented on cultural understanding and how girls' lives, in different countries, were similar or different. When Andrea and Samantha told me about it, I could see their pride and the lightbulbs of ideas flashing on as they spoke. "It's not yet big enough. Next year we want to do it even better!"

As Girl Scouts' leadership journeys show, vision is crucial to leadership. Vision is the source of your commitment: the true passion you have for what you are doing, and your willingness to offer your all. Vision prompts questions like: "What is our potential, moving forward? How much better can we be? What else is out there for us to achieve?"

An effective leader not only sees where she's trying to go, she also believes—she *knows*—she's going to get there. She is an optimist. If a CEO doesn't believe the goal can be accomplished, and if she doesn't say, "Yes, we can!" over and over and over, the job probably won't get done.

Not a Solo Act

Girl Scouts' transformation and our *Discover, Connect, Take Action* journeys have confirmed a major leadership lesson: leaders generally don't get big ideas all on their own. Leadership isn't all about being the one calling the shots. If I had come to GSUSA in 2003 with a fixed personal agenda as CEO, we couldn't possibly have gotten to where we are now. Having vision and confidence doesn't mean you have all the answers. If you put a leader in a room alone, don't expect her to come out with solutions to all your problems. But if you put a leader with a team of other impassioned folks, ideas will start to flow, particularly if the people in the group have different viewpoints. Gems of clarity arise in the mix of thoughts and ideas and possibilities and connections and patterns.

It may seem unsettling to hear a CEO to say, "I thrive on chaos," but this is where the best creative thinking and solutions come from.

Patience

Jim Collins says, "Vision without execution is hallucination." Yet execution sometimes takes a long, long time. You've got to be willing to give it enough time to prove whether it's working. This requires patience. You can't just send up a flare and hope the cavalry rides in. As much as we'd like to see quick fixes for Girl Scouts of the USA, and for girls in general, our transformation is far from done, and we need to see it through.

This is going to take a while. That's frustrating, because the United States has become an instant-gratification culture. But organizations that succeed in the long run do so by stepping back and considering where they want to go in the next 10 or 20 years. Part of achieving long-term success is to help folks understand that sometimes you have to endure short-term pain for the sake of long-term gain. Those who thrive in the long term develop patience to make long-range plans and stick with them. You've got to believe in the eventual payoff.

A powerful example is Girl Scouts' commitment to dedicate our energies to transformation at full steam even though we knew it would divert our attention from growing our membership. When I came aboard in 2003, girl membership had already been declining for a few years. In any nonprofit membership organization, a top priority always is to grow membership, especially if members' dues are a big revenue source to your operations. Girl Scouts' national board of directors understood that if we focused internally on trans- formation, we'd have less energy to reach out for membership and the numbers would keep declining, maybe even faster. Yet the board had the courage to pour our effort into moving ahead on all five priorities of our new core business strategy. They were confident that through our improved leadership program activities, the public's appreciation of our new brand, better delivery by high-capacity councils, and new flexible ways for girls and volunteers to take part, Girl Scouting would become much more attractive to girls.

Girl Scout membership has declined from a high of nearly three million girls in the mid-1990s to 2.4 million today. Yet our long-term patience is about to pay off: today we're becoming a more vital and exciting experience for girls than ever before, and the sky is the limit to how many girls soon will say, "I want to be a Girl Scout!"

Communication, Trust, and Self-Awareness

One other truth has emerged again and again in this transfor- mation process. It's the relationship of communication and trust. As a leader, you've got to communicate, communicate, communicate. There is no such thing as communicating too much. You have to resist a temptation to assume, "Okay, they've got it now." Instead you constantly need to be think- ing, "If I don't pass on critical information to people who know it's out there somewhere, they'll start to believe I don't trust them enough to handle it." If they think you don't trust them, they'll stop trusting you.

So you have to tell people what's going on. You have to tell them where you're coming from. You have to tell them where you're trying to go. Leaders sometimes hesitate to share the whole truth with everyone in the organization, feeling that it has to be packaged just right before it goes out. But speaking the truth is always the best thing, even when it's hard to do.

Girl Scouts' reinvigoration could never have gone as smoothly as it has if we hadn't constantly, consciously, built trust through sharing information. It is perhaps the second most important lesson we've learned from the whole experience: you can never overcommunicate. You must keep opening channels to listen, and to share what you hear, and to help everyone make sense of the whirlwind of information and opinions. It may be important to put things in a way that doesn't sound negative or scared (even if you secretly feel that way once in a while), but you have to keep talking and you have to tell the truth.

What's the first most important lesson? It's about the crucial leap between knowing something and *really* knowing it. For example, if you own a car, you know it's important to wear your seat belt and maintain the brakes and tires. You understand it intellectually. Then one day you're on the freeway doing 70 and all of a sudden you come around a curve and there's a stalled truck in your lane and nowhere for you to go and you slam on the brakes and manage to keep the car under control and not hit the truck and you pull over safely to the side of the road and you're sitting there with your hands shaking—that's when you *really* understand about seat belts and brakes and tires. That's when you really get it.

As measurable evidence of successful girl outcomes is coming in from our volunteers, our girls, and our scientific behavior studies, we at Girl Scouting are really getting that our model of the Girl Scout leadership experience—*Discover, Connect, Take Action*—truly works. Our new program is on the right track. If we who lead the girls can consistently demonstrate courage, confidence, and character—if we believe in our program, and if we always walk the talk in our interactions with girls, families, and donors—we *will* guide our girls to become leaders who make this world a better place.

9 Shaking the Money Tree

One of Girl Scouts' five core strategic priorities is fund development. As we started transforming our movement, we had to put our first attention into restructuring the council network, designing and rolling out our new girl program, and building Girl Scouts' brand as the country's best leadership experience for girls. Those things had to be in place before we could tackle the challenge to build a culture of philanthropy within our organization and a public awareness that girls are a top strategic investment.

Fund development is on our front burner now. And the need is pressing. Even when our traditional revenue streams recover from the recession, we'll need much wider donor support to achieve our new, more ambitious leadership goals for our current girls and the millions more to come.

Meanwhile, young people in this country are facing serious challenges. Obesity and related health issues in both girls and boys are spiraling. Thirty-five percent of African American and Hispanic kids in the United States live in poverty. The high school dropout rate averages 25 percent nationwide but it's as high as 50 to 75 percent in many urban school districts.

These problems affect girls and boys differently. Here are three startling examples. Male high school dropouts tend to be out on the streets; female high school dropouts, over-whelmingly, tend to be at home taking care of their families. Teen pregnancy happens only to girls (boys can, and often do, walk away), which typically sets off another cycle of poverty. And because girls tend to have lower self-esteem than boys have, their career aspirations are lower, which contributes to the fact that the majority of Americans holding minimum-wage jobs are women, and 80 percent of people living in poverty are women and their children.

Both girls and boys need help, but they need different kinds of help, a fact widely overlooked by donors and policy makers.

I'll keep saying this, at the risk of boring you: a serious change for the better in our society is going to hinge on improving the lot of girls. It isn't the only thing we need to do, but it is one thing we must do or nothing else we do is going to work right.

A Question of Priority

If girls are in this much trouble and if girls are a key to national leadership strength, you'd think girls' welfare would be a major focus of philanthropy in the United States. Yet it isn't. Girl-funding expert Nancy Gibbs reports that less than two cents of each development dollar, worldwide, goes to girls. (Gibbs's essay "To Fight Poverty, Invest in Girls" in *Time* magazine, February 14, 2011, aims a spotlight on girls in developing countries, but her message rings clear in the United States, too.) "And that is a victory compared with a few years ago when it was more like half a cent. Roughly nine out of ten youth programs are aimed at boys.[1] One

---

[1] Or programs target generic youth, which, in most cultures, tends to mean the same thing.

reason for this is that when it comes to lifting up girls, we don't know as much about how to do it. We have to start listening to girls, which much of the world is not culturally disposed to do. Development experts say the solutions need to be holistic, providing access to safe spaces, schools, and health clinics with programs designed specifically for girls' needs. Success depends on infrastructure, on making fuel and water more available so girls don't have to spend as much as fifteen hours a day fetching them. It requires enlisting whole communities—mothers, fathers, teachers, religious leaders—in helping girls realize their potential instead of seeing them as dispensable or, worse, as prey."

Nonmembers of the Tribe

In the United States, most girls don't have to spend hours every day carrying firewood and water. But they're still a long way from realizing their full potential. (They're also, at times, regarded both as dispensable and as prey.) They face problems that are inextricably bound up with being girls.

Philanthropy in our country doesn't make a priority of providing resources to solve those problems. A big reason why philanthropy doesn't focus on girls is that the huge majority of Americans in a position to solve problems are men. Philanthropic organizations are largely run by men. (Women make up nearly 75 percent of staff in the nonprofit sector; but the farther up the ladder you go, the more heavily male the decision making is.) Private giving also is driven primarily by men. Any woman who has tried to do fund development in an American community—for example, every Girl Scout council CEO—is aware that a vast number of the commitments and decisions around donating money get made on golf courses and in clubhouses and locker rooms and other venues that are overwhelmingly if not exclusively male.

This isn't a conspiracy on the part of men; it's just human nature. Suppose there's somebody you see two or three times a month. You have informal conversations and an occasional drink together. You tell each other jokes and compare notes on politics and the state of the world. If that person encourages you to support a good cause and you're in a position to write a substantial check, you are more likely to do it than if you're asked by someone who is less a part of your life and your social circle. In the United States, most people in a position to write those checks are men. The golf buddies they write them to also are men. This is tribal behavior, and we're not likely to change it.

Still, women have two good opportunities to generate funds for girls' programs. One is to keep making progress on getting more women into the ranks of the highly paid, to the point where those women can form their own tribal relationships. Another solution, which Juliette Low seems to have understood from the start, is to be creative in building revenue streams outside of standard channels.

Girl Scouting was born and grew up in an era when few women had their own money or bank accounts or valuable properties. Women of that era had little experience with money or the power to wield it, so generally they were uncomfortable trying to raise funds. Yet Girl Scouts' founding mothers had the courage to think big, and they came up with entrepreneurial, self-generating sources of revenue to grow Girl Scouting and keep the movement financially strong.

They set in place a system of national membership dues. They created Girl Scout merchandise and program resources that not only provide great programs and identity for the movement but also generate income. Their top marketing stroke of genius was the Girl Scout cookie sale, the most successful national marketing endeavor of any nonprofit organization.

The resourceful women who built these income streams ensured the growth of a multimillion-dollar organization at a time when very few women were in the workforce. But their effort fell short of establishing a culture of philanthropy in which women could be comfortable to ask for contributions, and where women could make a strong case for donors to support Girl Scouts, and where women could develop networks to bring major charitable giving to the movement.

A Culture of Philanthropy

A hundred years later, we are seriously trying to create a culture of philanthropy in our organization and among those who can contribute to the welfare of girls. We are coming full circle to the spirit of Juliette Low: in Girl Scouts' very early days, when the budding movement needed an infusion of cash, Juliette took off her prized family-heirloom strand of pearls and sold it and invested the money into Girl Scouting, and she encouraged other women to do likewise. Today everyone who works to support girls' and women's issues needs to be as creative as Girl Scouts' early leaders in looking for ways to raise funds.

We need to build relationships with private donors and explain to them what's at stake. This progress is slow, because building relationships takes time. We need to get the word out to the corporate sector about the importance of supporting girls and women, not out of justice or high-mindedness but because it makes good economic sense. This case was highlighted in an article a few years ago in *The Economist* ("The Importance of Sex," April 12, 2006). Noting that parents still often prefer to have boy children, on the basis that boys likely will be better providers for the parents' old age, *The Economist* said, "Girls may now be a better investment. Girls get better grades in school than boys; and in developed countries, more women than men go to university. Women are more likely to provide sound advice on investing their parents' nest egg: surveys show that women consistently achieve higher financial returns than men do. Furthermore, the increase in female employment has been the main driving force in growth in the past couple of decades."

Women, the article goes on to say, have contributed more to global gross domestic product (GDP) growth than new technology (including the Internet) or the rise of China and India. And women have much more to contribute. "To an economist, women are the world's most under-utilized resource; getting more of them into work is part of the solution to many economic woes, including shrinking populations and poverty."

Tomorrow's Scientists

The Economist notes that more women graduate from college in the United States now than men do. Yet relatively few women get degrees in the STEM fields: science, technology, engineering, and math. Earlier we discussed jumping-off

points, often very early in a girl's educational life, when she
may close the door forever on a STEM career. Girl Scouts
is having success in getting girls safely past those points and
keeping them on track through middle school and high
school. Girl Scout programs in science, technology, engineering, and math now inspire girls toward over half of all
our awards. The corporate sector, and the national economy
overall, needs girls to choose careers in STEM fields. The U.S.
Department of Labor says that by the time today's girls
graduate from college, the United States will need three million more scientists and engineers than it has today. To make
the numbers work, a lot more of those technical experts will
have to be women.

Girl Scouts is fueling that pipeline. For example, we partner with the Society of Women Engineers, Lockheed Martin,
Women in Technology, NASA, and many others to give girls
firsthand experience in building robots, conducting research
in marine biology, and winning science fair competitions.

Pam Lund, CEO of the Girl Scout Council of Eastern
Washington and Northern Idaho, recently had this exchange
with an international energy company in her region:

"How many engineers a year do you hire?"

"About four hundred."

"Are they easy to find?"

"No, they are not. It's a problem."

"And how many of your applicants are women?"

"Hardly any."

Pam told this firm, "This is not a short-term problem,
and I don't have a short-term solution for you. I do, however,

have a long-term solution. You make a 20-year strategic investment in us, and at the end of that time, Girl Scouts you're investing in will be your engineers and they'll solve your problem."

The firm wrote the council a check for $3.4 million.

A Billion Dollars for Girls

Fund-raising strategies like what Pam Lund's council and other Girl Scout councils all over the country are doing, coupled with GSUSA courting national donors, plus GSUSA and high-capacity councils partnering together to solicit big regional funders, will help the Girl Scout movement achieve its most ambitious fund development campaign ever. (Well, it'll be our most ambitious *so far*. We'll aim even higher in the future.) Our goal is to celebrate Girl Scouts' hundredth anniversary by raising a billion dollars over a five-year period, 2012 to 2016.

I remember the first time that number was spoken in our planning sessions. It was a late-night meeting. We were thinking incrementally, trying to come up with the right goal for our anniversary campaign. A consultant was with us, who had led a large and successful campaign for Oxford University. He asked, "How much have you been raising annually in the past?"

The answer is complicated. Each council sets its own budget and annual goals, and raises its own funds. In the years before our councils merged, smaller councils had an especially tough time doing that. For example, when I was council CEO in Greeley, Colorado, with six staff serving 3,500 girls and

1,000 adult volunteers, the council had no finance or fund development officer so I squeezed in budgeting and fund-raising while running all over the place doing everything else.

Still, even with this underdeveloped skill set, Girl Scout councils at the start of our transformation were collectively raising $130 million a year from corporate and private philanthropy in their local jurisdictions and from their cookie sales. And GSUSA was bringing in $10 million more via corporate partnerships and federally supported outreach programs. Over a five-year period—if the newly merged high-capacity councils met their marks—the whole organization could anticipate raising $700 million.

The consultant calmly said, "Why can't you do a billion?"

A billion! Immediately we all jumped up and said, "Yes!" Nobody said, "There's no way we could possibly do that." Instead, energy flowed through the room. The mark was set for discussions to come: a billion-dollar campaign for girls. In that moment, we turned a corner.

We could hardly wait to talk to the councils about it. Of course, buy-in from the councils would be essential. We couldn't just call them up and say, "Here's what's going to happen." Girl Scouting doesn't work that top-down way. To raise a billion dollars, a huge number of women would need to be spreading the Girl Scout story and coordinating with each other and with headquarters to approach donors. All the councils would need to unify with GSUSA to speak with a consistent voice and to team up for big requests.

Having a billion-dollar goal is healthy for our movement. It makes us focus and plan more effectively. It builds strong partnership between councils and GSUSA. Our inspiring, audacious goal says to customers and peers and funding sources, "We are leading the charge for girls."

When we meet this billion-dollar goal, we'll set a new philanthropic standard for, and by, girls and women in the United States and around the world. This campaign will change the way girls are seen as leaders. It will change the way women see themselves as donors and as fund-raisers. It will bring girls front and center as a crucial investment.

The Year of the Girl

One impetus to launch our Girl Scout campaign is our centennial anniversary. We've talked a lot about turning 100 years old, and we're proud that Girl Scouts has positively influenced the lives of more than 50 million girls over the past century. But the real point of our campaign is the great need, right now, that girls have for our support and that the country has for the leadership potential of girls.

As part of this campaign, we're inviting other girls' and women's organizations to join us in declaring 2012 to be the Year of the Girl. Together we aim to make the case for supporting girls so clear and compelling that it becomes a major, well-understood, and highly sought out focus of strategic charitable funding throughout the nonprofit sector, not just in the United States but around the world.

The campaign will make it clear to governments, businesses, foundations, and families how important girls' leadership development is to everyone's future. We will drive home the point that—recession or not—support for girls is a critical need and a powerfully effective investment in the United States.

10 Girl Scout, Phone Home

We're living in a time of enormous change. Were you as transfixed as I was, in the spring of 2011, by the images of grassroots democracy coming out of some of the Arab nations—countries that many of us thought were the most politically and socially unchanging on the globe? It was amazing and inspiring to see hundreds of thousands of ordinary people stand up and say, "Enough! Things have to change, and we don't mean in 20 years; we mean *now*."

How will those changes play out? Where will they take us? No one can be sure yet. But it's not likely that things in those nations are just going to go back to the way they were.

I'm particularly struck by women's actions in the uprisings in Cairo and Tunis and other cities caught up in this political and social whirlwind. At least for the moment, women are standing beside men in the public square, raising their voices against an oppressive past and for a better future.

Imagine how transfixing it would be in the United States if women here spoke with equal vigor on behalf of girls. "It's time! Things have to change, and we don't mean by dribs and drabs over the next few decades. We mean *now*."

Dribs and drabs aren't working. As I write this, a brand-new report has just come out. In honor of International Women's Day's hundredth anniversary, consulting firm Grant Thornton International has published a study on the status of women in leadership at top private companies worldwide. The report tells us that in 2011, only 20 percent of leaders in private companies worldwide are women. That's down from 24 percent in 2010. The largest economies—the G7 nations, including the United States—average 16 percent women leaders. Instead of seeing the current recession as an opportunity to reevaluate and refine operations, companies in these nations are reverting to a "play it safe" mentality instead.

This Is Safety?

But what they are trying to revert to is not safe.

The catastrophic 2011 earthquake and tsunami in Japan killed tens of thousands, displaced 10 times more, and crippled a major nuclear power plant. This nuclear plant had supposedly been designed to withstand such ravages; but four reactors are destroyed, risking severe radioactive contamination.

A major Girl Scout conference of senior staff from GSUSA and the CEOs of all our 112 councils happened to open four days after the earthquake. One of our speakers, Sally Helgesen, an international consultant on business management and gender issues—whose book *The Female Advantage* (Doubleday, 1990) is a classic study of the role and potential of women in management—commented that perhaps the most intransigently male-dominated and female-unfriendly group of companies she had ever dealt with was the Japanese utilities industry.

It's not unreasonable to wonder if the decisions made decades ago to put nuclear power plants atop the fracturing junction of Earth's tectonic plates would have been made the same way if women had sat at the utilities' leadership table.

In 2008 the global economy came close to meltdown at the hands of industries whose leaders proved miserably incapable of controlling the forces at their disposal. Is it coincidence that these industries, too, are almost completely dominated by men? Has anyone learned anything from watching these alleged leaders furiously try to pretend that nothing went wrong, and attempt to re-create the dysfunctional system that so recently collapsed?

Seizing the Decade

When you look at this and at the Grant Thornton report, you see the world trying to go backward. Well, we have seen where we came from, and it is not safe there. So what else can we do?

I mentioned that Girl Scouting is spearheading a nonprofit-sector celebration of 2012 as the Year of the Girl. But what we really need is a Decade of the Girl, because we need to take a giant step, and we need more than a year to do it.

When I was a young girl, Americans were afraid that our nation was falling behind in the new era of space exploration. Then President John F. Kennedy stood up and said we would put a man on the moon by the end of the decade. And we did. This is the kind of astonishing progress we are capable of. We have the ability to—and we need to—make the same great leap of progress in leadership parity within the coming 10 years. We need to put women (not just *some* women, but *enough* women) in every boardroom, on every executive team, and within every center of power in the nation. We have tried tokenism, and it doesn't work. And it isn't enough for women to just be close enough to hear the conversation; we have to be within it, in order to change it.

It is going to take work. Look around you at the girls who are age 8, 9, and 10, and at the high school girls just now earning their Girl Scout Gold Award and learning how the world works. They are our leaders of the future. We need to lift them up. We need to put the equivalent of a moon rocket under those girls and boost them into the vital challenges of leadership.

Crossing the Bridge

Remember the Girl Scout bridging ceremonies? Imagine a worldwide bridging ceremony. On one side of the bridge are millions upon millions of girls, getting ready to cross. They are of all ages, all sizes and shapes, some bold, some curious, some nervous. They're figuring out who they are. Imagine the anticipation hanging in the air, the promise of more and better to come.

Now imagine the other side of that bridge. That's the future. Over there is a world in which men and women lead together in a balanced, respectful way. Over there, girls and women are valued not just for what they look like or the things they do that are cute, but for their intelligence, skill, compassion, humor, strength, and even their power.

What do you think this bridge is made of?

It's made of people like you and me. It's made of a father who wants a better future for his daughter. A college-aged young woman who has some extra time and wants to give back to her community. A corporate executive who has noticed that the company and its leadership are not as woman-friendly as they could be. An artisan who wants to pass on her skills. A scientist who wants to encourage others to know the joy of hard study. A philanthropist seeking a cause. Someone who works in an organization that helps adult women to link arms with others. The bridge to the future, for millions of girls, is not some fantasy that can't be built. The bridge is simply us.

Let's Make It Happen

Moon rockets don't come for free, and neither do bridges. We can't just see the potential of a new world. We can't just want it. We have to make it happen.

Let me tell you some ways Girl Scouts is making it happen. This may inspire you to join us, and that's good: we need your help. If you're a parent, and you think your daughter might enjoy and benefit from the things we've been talking about, please get in touch with the Girl Scout council that serves your area. Wherever you are, we're nearby. We're in every zip code in the United States, and on military bases and in American and international schools in about 90 countries. Call 800-247-8319 or check us out at www.girlscouts.org.

Here's another option for you: become a Girl Scout volunteer. You'll be joining a million dedicated adults who apply their talents in dozens of important ways, from the national board of directors (yes, they're volunteers) to working directly with girls in every Girl Scout council. This million-woman corps makes it possible to deliver the Girl Scout leadership to our 2.4 million girls. And of course in the near future, when we hope our new program of leadership journeys will attract twice as many girls, we'll need a million new volunteers like you.

Volunteers can make a crucial impact in the lives of girls. For example, a year or so ago, a seven-year-old Brownie Girl Scout, whose family was stationed overseas while her father was deployed in Iraq, lost her mother in childbirth. When the girl got the news from the hospital, the first person she called was her troop leader. "Mrs. Beebe, my mommy is dead. I need you." It was her troop leader, and her sister Girl Scouts, whom she stayed with and who comforted her until her father could return from Iraq.

A Smoother Pathway

As important as our volunteers are, we haven't always made the volunteer experience as smooth or easy as it should be. Some women (and men; our male volunteers, who do a wonderful job, often wear T-shirts that say, "Are you man enough to be a Girl Scout?") have tried to join as volunteers but they came away from the attempt frustrated.

Maybe it happened to you. Maybe you were told that if you volunteered, you had to be a troop leader; but you didn't have the time to commit to that. If so, please get back in touch with us. We're building many new ways for people with limited time but unlimited passion to contribute to the lives of girls.

You may have felt that if you're not the mother of an elementary school girl, you can't fit in as a Girl Scout volunteer. That's far from true. Mothers are the backbone of our volunteer service to their daughters and their daughters' friends; but we also need women of any life experience, to lend a hand

and be role models. We need the energy of young women—in college, or early in their careers—who want to work with and encourage girls only a few years younger than themselves. And we're finding these volunteers, because we're making it easier for you to find us and for you to integrate your life and your gifts into what we do for girls. So if we've ever discouraged you—or if you've ever looked at Girl Scouts and thought, "That doesn't look like me"—try us again. Let us invigorate your life with new challenges, new training, new leadership skills, and the delight of doing great things for girls.

Going Where Others Won't

If you want to go where the need is really great, here are a couple of Girl Scout programs you may not be aware of.

Girl Scouts Beyond Bars was established in 1992 in partnership with the National Institute of Justice. This program serves girls who have an incarcerated parent—including many mothers. From 1995 to 2005, the number of women in prisons grew by more than half, and three out of four are mothers. As of 2007, 1.7 million children in the United States—that's one in 43—had a parent in jail or in prison.[1] It's not uncommon for these children to show signs of post-traumatic stress disorder. They deal with social stigma, shame, abandonment, anger, potential addiction, and impaired ability to deal with stress. Without stable role models, they're frighteningly vulnerable, and in danger of going down the same road as their parents.

---

[1]National Resource Center on Children and Families of the Incarcerated.

Girl Scouts Beyond Bars lessens the impact of separation between the girls and their imprisoned mothers. We've had programs in more than 20 facilities over the years, with meetings taking place at least twice a month. One of those meetings is a mother/daughter troop meeting at the facility, where mothers and daughters take part in both planning and carrying out program activities. There also may be discussions for the mothers about conflict resolution, drug and violence prevention, financial planning, and healthy family life. Once the mothers are released, those families can continue to take part in Girl Scouting activities in their communities.

Imagine the girl who feels alone in having a mother in prison. Imagine her not being able to deal with her feelings of embarrassment and confusion. Now imagine that same girl seeing her mother in a leadership role, gaining self-confidence and skills in the same way she is.

There are variations on the Girl Scouts Beyond Bars program. A troop may include the caretaker families who watch over the children in the parents' absence. Another troop may incorporate fathers in male correctional facilities. Another troop, realizing that not all girls can visit a parent in prison, pairs those girls with adult mentors to help them grow and thrive despite their circumstances.

A Girl Scout troop in Austin, Texas, produced *Troop 1500,* a vivid documentary on our Girl Scouts Beyond Bars program. We can make that film available to you—it may inspire you to lend your time and your heart to this project.

Girls in Trouble

It's not just adult women who end up behind bars. The fastest-growing population group in juvenile detention centers is girls between the ages of 10 and 17. Girl Scouting in Detention Centers, which began in the 1990s, is the only gender-specific program in the country that aims to help these girls develop the inner leadership to overcome their mistakes. Our program has been praised by detention authorities and girl participants for building girls' sense of self and relationship with the world under extremely difficult circumstances. In 2010 the program served nearly 2,500 girls nationwide.

"For some girls," says a Girl Scout project manager in northern California, "the impact is immediate. These are the girls that don't come back to the center once they leave. When you run into them at the mall or at the movies, they stop to tell you they're still clean and doing well, or back in school and taking it seriously, or working at a 'real' job."

Once a Girl Scout, Always a Girl Scout

A group that we're really eager to be involved with in our next century of growth is former Girl Scouts. For a lot of reasons (which we're now correcting), our record keeping has been spotty to nonexistent, so we need you to find us. We want to help you become a big part of the bridge that spans the gap from where Girl Scouting is to where our girls need us to be. If you've ever worn brown or green with your sisters, if you've ever sold cookies, if we've touched you in the past, we want you back.

So, Girl Scout, phone home. Go to www.girlscouts.org, click the alumnae button, and let us hear from you. Today.

We know you're out there, and we know you've still got the Girl Scout spirit. For example, a lively lady whom I see every year at a music festival in south Texas has kept in touch with her troop (they have a reunion every year) for more than half a century. Hey, Pokey: phone home!

Recently at the historic Great Hall at our Macy Conference Center, Girl Scouts held a reunion of women in their eighties and nineties who had earned the Girl Scout Golden Eaglet award in their teens. (That's what the Gold Award used to be called.) The women were honored, excited, and rich with memories. Hey, Golden Eaglets: phone home!

Alumnae or not, we want to hear from you. If you're a girl, or if you ever were a girl, or if you care about a girl, and you'd like to work—in any capacity—to make the world a better place for girls, we want to hear from you. Hey, girls: phone home!

If you'd rather work on your own or through other organizations, that's great, too. While you're doing that, we always welcome you to get in touch with Girl Scouts for support, or for information about girls' and women's issues through our Girl Scout Research Institute.

We as a country, and girls as a gender, *need your help*. The need is urgent and it's vast—way, way bigger than Girl Scouts. We'll take the lead where we can, because girls and leadership are what Girl Scouting is all about. But we're eager to share this struggle with anyone who wants to get involved. The prize is worth the effort. Girls are tough cookies; but they aren't tough enough, all by themselves, to create the world we need for them to live in. It's time for the rest of us to stand up and help them.

ABOUT the AUTHOR

The wall-to-wall reinvention of a successful, 100-year-old iconic organization can be risky business. But Girl Scouts of the USA CEO Kathy Cloninger stepped into her running shoes and engaged thousands of staff, volunteers, and girls in remaking Girl Scouts into America's go-to expert and advocate on girls' and women's issues, and the premier leadership experience for millions of girls ages 5 to 17.

The child of a working-class home in Dallas, Texas, Ms. Cloninger paid her way through college with tips she earned as a waitress, and then followed her heart through every step of a remarkable career that has put her finger on the pulse of America's girls and America's need for women to lead at every level.

For Cloninger, Girl Scouts' new leadership program and brand, and its powerful impact on diverse girls and communities, creates a vital "leadership pipeline" toward better balance in American decision making—and a better world.

Cloninger Serves As:

- Chair, the National Collaboration for Youth.
- Secretary of the board, National Assembly of Human Services.

- National board, American Humanics.
- National board, National Council for Research on Women.
- Advisory board, America's Promise.
- Executive committee, Leadership 18.
- Founder, Tennessee's Association of Nonprofit Executives.

Awards:

- Nonprofit CEO of the Year 2000, Center for Nonprofit Management.
- 2000 NCCJ Human Relations Award.
- 2007, 2008, and 2009 *Nonprofit Times* Power & Influence Top 50.
- 2010 "21 Leaders for the 21st Century," *Women's eNews.*
- 2011 Honorary Doctor of Letters degree, Texas A&M University

Cloninger and songwriter husband Michael share a love of country music. Together they have hosted 350 world-class songwriter concerts in their homes in Nashville and New York.

INDEX